A Climbing Guide To Colorado's Fourteeners

A Climbing Guide To Colorado's Fourteeners

Updated Second Edition

By Walter R. Borneman and Lyndon J. Lampert

PRUETT **P** PUBLISHING COMPANY
Boulder, Colorado

Library of Congress Cataloging-in-Publication Data

Borneman, Walter R., 1952-
   A climbing guide to Colorado's fourteeners / by Walter R. Borneman and Lyndon J. Lampert. — 2nd ed.
      p   cm.
   Includes index.
   ISBN 0-87108-751-0
   1. Mountaineering — Colorado — Guide-books.
   2. Backpacking — Colorado — Guide-books.
   3. Colorado — Description and travel — 1981-   — Guide-books.
   I. Lampert, Lyndon J., 1956-
   II. Title.
GV199.42.C6B67   1988
917.88 — dc 19   88-28789
                                                            CIP

Second Edition

1 2 3 4 5 6 7 8 9

Printed in the United States of America.

Front Cover Photograph
Wilson Peak — Courtesy of Gary Koontz

Photographs not otherwise credited, by Walter R. Borneman.

Design & Typography
Shadow Canyon Graphics   Evergreen, Colorado

Contents

Acknowledgements

Part of the joy of mountaineering is in the companionship of those friends who travel the trail with you. Preparing this second edition has revived many memories of grand times gone by and we gratefully acknowledge our many friends — old and new — who have shared the ecstacy of at least one summit with us, as well as the many people who provided assistance and photographs: Omar and Anne Richardson and their children Naomi and Nathaniel, Gary and Dolora Koontz, Craig and Debbie Koontz, Tim Duffy, Duane Vandenbusche, Ron Pierce, Dave Hunter, Dave Huntley, Bob Hooper, Adam Csoeke-Poechk, David Younger, Brian Baird, Steve Richardson, Bill Salisbury, Richard, Sadie, and Steve Taylor, Ken and Lois Lampert, Jasper Welch, John Chesley, Eleanor Gehres and the staff of the Western History Department of the Denver Public Library, Maxine Benson and the staff of the Colorado Historical Society, Jim Pruett, Jerry Keenan, and the staff of Pruett Publishing Company, John L. Jerome Hart, Stephen H. Hart, Carl Blaurock, William M. Bueler, Robert F. Rosebrough, Dan Roberts, Phil Schmuck, Glen Gebhardt, Robert Ormes, and "Skipper," who could claim six Fourteeners by his first birthday.

In our first edition, a special thanks went to Jim Gehres, who then had climbed all of Colorado's Fourteeners at least four times. Jim devoted many hours to reviewing our maps and route descriptions. In the ten years since then, our respect for Jim's accomplishments and our appreciation for his continuing critique of this guide are exceeded only by his own achievements. At this 1988 writing, Jim has climbed almost all of the Fourteeners nine times, and no one doubts that he will soon reach his goal of ten climbs of each 14,000-foot summit. Jim's input to this second edition was characteristically thorough. With those who suggest that Jim Gehres should have written this guide in the first place, we can only agree wholeheartedly! Thanks, Jim!

Lastly, warm thanks go to our companion of so many miles and summits, R. Omar Richardson.

*To tomorrow's climbers,
in the hope that our responses
to the challenges of today
will preserve for them
a wilderness legacy.*

Preface to Second Edition

When the first edition of *A Climbing Guide To Colorado's Fourteeners* appeared in 1978, we wrote with concern about a state and its wonderful mountains on the threshold of dramatic change. A decade later, our concern has both matured and deepened. Some of the environmental issues of the 1970s — rampant boom town construction in search of energy resources and recreation complexes gone wild — have, for a time, eased. Other issues, such as the omnipresent quest for re-allocation of finite water resources and the task of transporting more and more people about, remain at the forefront.

Interwoven with these issues of mega-impacts on our natural environment are the smaller but more personally poignant ones in increasing evidence on every 14,000-foot summit. Today's well-worn trail into the Pyramid Peak amphitheater was difficult at best, bushwhacking at worst, a decade ago. One could camp in Chicago Basin fifteen years ago without encountering another soul. Twenty years ago, the roar of jeeps on Mount Antero was restricted to below the Baldwin Gulch Creek crossing.

In bemoaning the hordes of people climbing Colorado's Fourteeners, some climbers have berated us for having written this guide. To be sure, we did not, as the other literature on the topic affirms, invent or even promote "the Fourteeners craze." And, to be sure, the mountains belong to us all, not to a few chosen early arrivals. This means, however, that along with the right to climb these mountains, goes the responsibility for their care.

With this second edition, we simply restate our personal philosophy of walking in harmony with the land and minimizing — to whatever extent possible — our impact on the mountains and waters we visit. Such an attitude will not of course resolve the larger issues or turn back the clock, but it may help slow the change and preserve a wilderness legacy for our children.

Once again, we have described the routes using the latest available information, but users of this guide are reminded that route information, particularly that of trailhead access, can change rapidly. *You assume full responsibility for using this information in a safe manner. This guide is not a substitute for your experience and common sense.*

Our goal is a third edition of this guide in another ten years which will be devoid of grim new accident statistics and stricter use regulations. If the mountains are to belong to us all, we must all share the responsibility for their care.

Prelude to High Adventure

Like the spiny backbone of an ancient dinosaur, the Colorado Rockies wind their jagged course through 300 miles of the roof of the continent, from the range country of Wyoming to the Spanish haciendas of New Mexico. Few geographic formations can boast the majestic beauty and rugged splendor of these mountains, and equally few have had such a profound influence on the peoples of the surrounding regions.

In an era when Colorado stands on the threshold of rapid change brought about by major challenges in water, energy, and almost unparalleled growth, one of the state's most precious resources remains the wilderness refuge of its mountains. Each year, in increasing numbers, people visit Colorado's high country.

If you are the intrepid climber who delights only in hanging for days on towering granite walls and counting one's progress in inches, then read no further. This book is not for you. Likewise, if you are the "great" American camper who packs up the wife, kids, and a case of beer and pulls a twenty-foot trailer up a mountain grade to a campground cluttered with similar souls, then also read no further. Neither is this book for you.

If, on the other hand, you count yourself in the rapidly growing number who swing packs on their backs and head out for a weekend of backpacking and climbing mountains, keep reading. You will be pleasantly surprised. This book fills a gap in Colorado climbing literature by providing the mountaineer a guide to the history and climbing routes of Colorado's fourteen-thousand-foot mountains — the Fourteeners.

The guide is by no means meant to be definitive either in routes or in history. By the same token, it is definitely not a "how-to" book for technique — others far more qualified have already told that story.

This book is, however, a resource of text, maps, and pictures for climbers to add to their experience and knowledge and make future climbs more interesting.

A word of caution! The mere acquisition of a guidebook does not make one a climber! Know your mountain and *know the limits of your experience and physical condition.* While most Colorado Fourteeners require little more technical ability than a pair of strong legs and strong lungs, knowledge of mountain safety is a necessity. Colorado climbers must be aware of the importance of watching mountain weather and being off the summit early to avoid lightning strikes. In addition, extra caution on loose rock slopes and snowfields is a must for safe travel, and ice axes may be necessary for some routes. A careless step on even Colorado's easiest Fourteener or an unheeded thunderstorm can spell disaster; *above all, climb with care and common sense.*

The mountain you set out to climb has been there for thousands of years. Chances are that it will still be there long after you are gone. Experienced climbers have tales by the dozens of aborting climbs within feet of the desired summit because of weather, avalanche danger, a party member's fatigue, or any conceivable situation which threatened the safety of the climbing team. The mountain will wait for another day. Do not push yourself beyond the limits of safety.

In presenting possible climbing routes, it is not the intent of this guide to provide a step-by-step description. Part of the fun and challenge of climbing is in route finding. Consequently, the route descriptions may suggest the north ridge of Torreys and warn of a particularly airy pitch one hundred feet below the summit, but not give a foot-by-foot description.

The route descriptions in this guide assume summer climbs from late spring until early fall unless specifically noted otherwise. The world of winter mountaineering offers unique challenges not found by the summer climber as well as the frequent satisfaction of having the mountain all to one's self. Many of the summer routes listed are climbable in winter by experienced parties. Here again, however, "experience" is the key word.

Finally, it seems impossible to begin a guidebook and history of great mountains without at least a passing reference to the age old question of why people climb mountains. There are those who would immediately quote the old cliche, "Because it is there," and others who climb to prove a point. In the final analysis, however, those who climb do so for a very personal reward and for the satisfaction of having met a very personal challenge. The most important reason for climbing should be because *you* want to. Because *you* want to endure the burning of lungs and the aching of legs long enough to capture the ecstacy of the final steps to the summit. Because *you* want to. Make sense? If so, throw this book in your pack and let's go!

Colorado Mountain Ranges

So Bold, So Beautiful A Land

The General Geography and Geology of Colorado

The magnificent Rocky Mountains are legendary — the mere mention of "the Rockies" conjures up vivid pictures of towering peaks, verdant forests, torrential rivers, and unspoiled wilderness. Also connected with the Rockies are less dramatic images of peaceful herds of grazing elk, trembling, golden aspen leaves, and the lone prospector and his burro. Undoubtedly, it is a combination of all of these factors which add up to what may be called "the mystique of the Rockies." Whatever the specific reasons, the Rockies well deserve their legendary status, and undoubtedly will hold a special place in the hearts of North Americans for countless generations to come.

A good portion of the Rockies' prominence and allure is due to their geographic dimensions. From the forbidding barrenness of the Brooks Range of northern Alaska, the Rockies sweep southward for more than 3,000 miles, terminating in the arid American Southwest in the vicinity of Santa Fe, New Mexico. Between these two points, the Rockies are mountains of incredible variety, but they are always impressive and frequently an imposing barrier to those desiring to cross them.

Indeed, the histories of both Canada and the United States have been significantly affected by the presence of the dominating Rockies. Besides being impressive as a very lengthy mountain chain, the Rockies have equally imposing vertical dimensions. Most Rocky Mountain summits average 8,000 to 12,000 feet above sea level, and it is understandable how the early traveler, accustomed to the rolling Appalachians, would be awed by the sight of snowy peaks rising up to 10,000 feet above the high plains. To be sure, it remains an impressive sight today.

The apex of the Rocky Mountain chain, the concentration

of its highest summits, lies in the state of Colorado, near the southern terminus of the Rockies. More than 1,500 Colorado points rise above 12,000 feet, and 637 separate summits reach above 13,000 feet. The elite of Colorado's mountains are the 54 peaks which surpass 14,000 feet — the Fourteeners. Colorado holds almost 80 percent of the 68 Fourteeners in the contiguous United States. California boasts 13, while Washington claims Mount Rainier. Truly, with such statistics considered, no state more deserves to be called "the crest of the continent" than does Colorado. Even with its many Fourteeners, however, it is an unfortunate assumption made by some that Colorado's only great peaks are its Fourteeners. In truth, many of the state's most spectacular and interesting peaks do not reach the 14,000-foot level and deserve more attention than is usually given them.

That Colorado is a state of multitudinous high peaks and vast expanses of rock and tundra is of no question, but to think of it solely as this would be a grave mistake. In reality, the Rockies cover only about the middle two-fifths of the state. To the east extends the immensity of the Great Plains, stretching for 150 miles to the Kansas border and then beyond. The importance of the plains to Colorado is often overlooked, but in truth they have historically provided a solid agricultural base for the state as well as the best transportation routes for those seeking to travel into Colorado's mountains. The plains gradually slope upward from about 3,500 to 5,000 feet, meeting the Rockies along a line of approximately 105° W longitude, roughly from Fort Collins to Trinidad. The contrast formed by the interface of the gentle plains meeting the sharply rising Rockies is significant, for other than proximity, the mountains and plains have little in common. Geography has led to contrasting histories, cultures, and atmospheres between the two areas.

Likewise, to the west of the Colorado Rockies lies a vast land quite unlike the mountains. This area may be termed the plateau and canyon region, and roughly occupies the western fifth of Colorado. Geographically, it is a part of the Colorado Plateau and is akin to the character of the great Southwest, complete with massive red cliffs towering above muddy rivers, and high, cool mesas, some reaching in excess of 11,000 feet. Like the plains, the plateau and canyon region has developed uniquely, quite differently from the mountains. Here, population is sparse, economy revolves around ranching and agriculture, and the culture has a decided Spanish flavor. Truly, Colorado is much more than "just mountains," and realizing this can be very enriching, even to those who are primarily attracted to its peaks.

Colorado's mountains, then, are only a part of the varied geography of the state, but it will probably always be the Rockies that first come to mind when one thinks of Colorado — and what mountains they are! Range upon majestic range line the central part of the state, each shimmering in the intense mountain sunlight, like vast numbers of pearls on a string. Most of Colorado's ranges are aligned north to south, paralleling each other, but the San Juans bulge extensively into the southwestern part of the state, providing the major exception to this north-south trend.

West of the impressive Front Range rise the Park and Gore ranges; neither contains any Fourteeners, but they are nonetheless every bit as rugged as Colorado's higher ranges. These two ranges are separated from the Front Range by North and Middle parks — large, relatively level basins which are ringed with peaks. South Park is the largest and most striking of Colorado's parks; it separates the Front Range from the Tenmile and Mosquito ranges, which are small ranges, but they contain five Fourteeners and are rich in mining history. The valley of the upper Arkansas River divides the Mosquito Range from Colorado's highest range, the Sawatch.

The Elk Range is somewhat a northwest spur of the Sawatch, but it is quite unlike any other Colorado range in terms of geology and the unique, layered character of its peaks. The Sangre de Cristo Range is long and narrow, stretching from the vicinity of Salida well into New Mexico. Last, but by no means least, the San Juans round out the roster of Colorado's major ranges, occupying a sizeable chunk of the southwestern part of the state. No two of Colorado's ranges are alike, and this variety offers ever-changing joys for the casual tourist, the photographer, the backpacker, and the climber.

It is impossible to discuss the geography of Colorado without mentioning the important element of water. The great "divider of the waters," the Continental Divide, winds through the heart of Colorado's mountains, making a great western bend as it travels through the San Juans. Most of Colorado's high peaks cluster near the Continental Divide, but the divide itself does not necessarily follow the highest ridges. Of 54 Fourteeners, only Grays and Torreys sit squarely on the Continental Divide.

Three of North America's great rivers originate deep within the Colorado Rockies — the Rio Grande, the Arkansas, and the Colorado. The importance of these rivers and the Colorado snowpack from which they are born is impossible to overestimate. The availability of water from these rivers is vital to the survival of large numbers of communities, farms, and ranches. Colorado is a semiarid land, and while the mountains receive a greater precipitation than the rest of the state, it is far less than in such ranges as the Cascades. Therefore, the Colorado Rockies are mountains of unique character, void of dense vegetation and large glaciers, but abounding with clear blue sky, and in winter, world-renowned, dry powder snow.

The individual ranges of the Colorado Rockies are of almost infinite variety — combinations of massive peaks, ragged ridges, flower-sprinkled meadows, sheltered valleys, serene lakes, and cascading streams. The mountains are much more than mere masses of rock; they are inseparably bound to their flora, fauna, weather, and water. Given this, any written description is bound to be inadequate, for only when one has actually climbed the peaks, traveled the valleys, breathed the mountain air, and personally experienced Colorado's mountains, does their full character truly come alive.

To fully grasp the character of the Colorado Rockies, something of the processes and forces that went into forming them must be understood. The geologic story of Colorado's mountains is a long and ancient one, beginning in the first era of geologic time, the Precambrian. During this era, most of the earth's "basement rocks" were formed in one of three ways. Igneous rocks are formed by the solidifying of molten rock from deep within the earth. Sedimentary rocks are formed by the accumulation and cementing together of eroded particles of other rocks, and are deposited by wind, streams, or oceans. Metamorphic rocks are formed when either igneous or sedimentary rocks are subjected to tremendous heat and pressure and are changed.

Much of Colorado was part of an ocean bed for at least a portion of the four-billion-year Precambrian Era. Underwater sedimentary deposits, eroded from the neighboring land, piled to depths of up to 40,000 feet, and the resultant pressure caused by such a thickness changed much of the sedimentary rock into metamorphic rock; the two most common types in Colorado are gneiss and schist. Later, forces from within the earth caused the bedrock to rise and the sea to retreat. This uplifting was accompanied by molten rock rising from within the earth and filling the cracks in the gneiss and schist. When this molten rock solidified, it formed granite, the igneous rock that is the third major type of Precambrian rock found in Colorado today.

The end of the Precambrian Era was a time of great erosion, and the upland of gneiss, schist, and granite in the Colorado region were eroded to a nearly level plain at sea level, and the area became highly susceptible to encroachments by the ever-changing seas. Indeed, during the next two eras of geologic history, the Paleozoic and Mesozoic, a combined span of 500 million years, the area was alternately invaded by the sea and then uplifted. Each time the sea encroached upon the land, a layer of sediment was deposited. These sediments became cemented together and formed many of the sandstones and shales found in Colorado.

About 70 million years ago, the sea retreated from Colorado for the last time. Causing this retreat was a great uplift of the entire Rocky Mountain chain; this uplift is called the Laramide Orogeny. This event ushered in the last geologic era, the Cenozoic, which is divided into two periods, the Tertiary, lasting from 70 million years ago to 3 million years ago, and the Quaternary, lasting from the end of the Tertiary to the present.

The Laramide Orogeny occupied the first half of the Tertiary Period, and it was during this time that most of Colorado's ranges as known today were formed. Mountain ranges of the Laramide Orogeny were formed in several different manners, but the most common in Colorado is the faulted anticline. The Front, Sawatch, Park, Gore, Tenmile, and Mosquito ranges are all examples of basically faulted anticline ranges. Anticlines are formed when forces within the earth cause flexible sedimentary layers of the earth's crust to be bent in a series of upward-arching corrugations, or anticlines. In Colorado, the lower layer of Precambrian gneiss, schist, and granite, being less flexible, was often lifted as a block below the sedimentary layers and broken rather than bent by these forces. When the Precambrian layer was broken, or faulted, along the edges of the uplift, a faulted anticline was produced.

The bent sedimentary layers, now considerably higher than the surrounding land, were immediately attacked by erosion. These soft layers were eroded away relatively quickly, leaving only the hard Precambrian core exposed. Therefore, many of Colorado's faulted anticline ranges are composed of a hard Precambrian core or "spine" of peaks which are flanked by upturned sedimentary layers, as is so vividly seen along the Front Range in such areas as the Flatirons near Boulder. While most of Colorado's ranges are faulted anticlines, there are some exceptions; the Elk, the northern Sangre de Cristo, and the San Juan ranges are the major ones. The geology of each of these ranges is discussed in the individual range introductions.

The uplifting and faulting of the Laramide Orogeny in Colorado was accompanied by flows of igneous rock from deep within the earth. Flows that cooled and solidified before reaching the surface are called intrusions; these are of two major types, batholiths and stocks. A batholith is a massive, blister-type formation which never quite reached the surface, but which may have become exposed later due to the erosion of overlying layers of rock. Stocks are similar in formation to batholiths but are smaller. Igneous flows which reached the surface and then solidified are known as extrusives or volcanics. Tertiary volcanism was most prevalent in the vicinity of the San Juans, and thus most San Juan peaks are composed of layers of volcanic rocks.

One important consequence of the Laramide Orogeny and associated Tertiary intrusions was the deposition of minerals in Colorado. The uplifting and intrusions caused mineral-rich solutions to seep into the many cracks in the rocks. These minerals, among them silver and gold, crystallized into veins, and eventually led to the development of Colorado as one of the important mineral producers of the West.

The Quaternary Period in Colorado, due to general climatic cooling, was characterized by the formation of immense mountain glaciers, reaching down the valleys as far as elevations of 8,000 feet. Because they were far south of the great continental ice sheets of this period, Colorado glaciers formed only in areas where the elevation and snowfall were great enough for the winter snow accumulation to exceed summer melting. These glaciers began near the crest of the ranges and slowly ground their way down valleys previously occupied by streams.

The glaciers had a dramatic effect on the landscape. They deepened valleys, steepened slopes, carved cirques, and deposited great masses of rock debris at their terminuses and along their edges; these debris accumulations are known as moraines. The effects of glaciation in Colorado are probably most strikingly seen in the great glacier-carved cirques of the Sawatch Range, the spectacularly polished east face of Longs Peak, and the ubiquitous alpine lakes that were frequently formed by glacial scouring of the bedrock.

Today, climatic conditions are too mild for the presence of large glaciers in Colorado. However, the Front Range contains a number of very small glaciers found in the most sheltered cirques, but these are leading only a marginal existence. Although there are a number of permanent snowfields and ice bodies in the other Colorado ranges, they cannot technically be called glaciers unless they move and show signs of that movement, such as crevasses.

It remains to be seen by future generations as to whether or not climatic conditions will cause great mountain glaciers to form once again in Colorado. In the meantime, the geologic story continues in the Colorado Rockies. Wind, water, and frost are at work in the mountains, slowly but constantly changing the physical nature of the peaks. The fact remains, too, that although the mountains appear to be permanent and unchanging, the geologic history of Colorado's mountains bears out that they are, in reality, a very dynamic part of the landscape.

Early Ventures
Into A Beckoning Land
History to 1860

Man first ventured into the labyrinth of the North American continent somewhere between 15,000 and 20,000 years ago. Nomadic bands crossed the land bridge linking Siberia and Alaska and slowly made their way across North America. Archaeological evidence suggests that descendants of these early inhabitants may have roamed the San Luis Valley as early as 8000 B.C. Yet, it was not until roughly the time of Christ that a people arrived in Colorado who would leave a definite legacy.

Gradually forsaking the nomadic wanderings of their ancestors, an Indian people settled on the mesas of southwestern Colorado and slowly adopted an agrarian life-style. Referred to as Basket Makers or as the "Anasazi," a Navajo word meaning "ancient ones," these people subsisted on small game and a variety of crops grown on the mesa tops. Their civilization culminated in the Classic Pueblo Period of 1100 to 1300 A.D., when the architectural masterpieces of Mesa Verde were constructed.

Venturing from their homes in Cliff Palace or Spruce Tree House, these cliff dwellers could stand on Mesa Verde's crest and gaze north into the heart of the San Juans. From the main settlements on Mesa Verde, hunters and traders ventured into the foothills of the range. Is it possible that an ultimate Anasazi manhood rite may have included a climb to the mountains now called the Wilsons and El Diente? If so, the bold adventurers' names have been lost to history.

By 1300, years of sustained drought and crop failures caused the Anasazi to abandon Mesa Verde and gradually migrate southward to be assimilated by the Pueblo tribes of the Southwest. Two centuries after the abandonment of Mesa Verde, an Italian seaman, under the auspices of the Spanish flag, sailed west from

Europe and, rather than falling off the edge of the earth as some notables of his day had predicted, explored a new world. Columbus' voyage sparked an age of exploration by the great powers of Europe, which by the early 1600s saw permanent colonies planted on three of the four corners of what would one day be the United States.

American history has frequently heralded the accomplishments of the French frontier of the St. Lawrence River Valley and the English frontier of the Atlantic seaboard while paying little or no attention to the third great power battling for empire in the New World. To be sure, Spain established the provincial capital of Santa Fe, New Mexico, in 1609, two years after the founding of Jamestown and a full eleven years before the Pilgrims' arrival at Plymouth Rock. Indeed, Santa Fe was but the northern fringe of a huge Spanish empire which stretched from Cape Horn to the Colorado and Rio Grande rivers and which dated from Cortes' conquest of the Aztecs in 1520.

While French and English fur traders pushed westward across the Appalachian Mountains and through the Great Lakes region, Spanish adventurers made repeated excursions into the lands north of Santa Fe. In 1706, Juan de Ulibarri reached the Arkansas River in southeastern Colorado and claimed its drainage for his Spanish majesty Philip V. Ulibarri confined his activities to the eastern plains and did not venture westward to explore the lands at the river's headwaters.

A dozen major Spanish expeditions traveled the eastern Colorado plains in the first half of the 1700s, searching for precious minerals, spreading Christianity, pursuing runaway slaves, and countering French fur-trader advances, but all stayed clear of the towering mountain ranges of central Colorado. However, while no documented report of Spanish exploration into Colorado's mountains prior to 1776 remains, there are evidences of mineral explorations to the La Plata Mountains and also abundant tales of lost mines and buried treasure in the Sangre de Cristo Range. Indeed, when Franciscan priests Francisco Dominguez and Silvestre Escalante led their small band of adventurers through southwestern Colorado in 1776, they were following a well-established trail of prior Spanish exploration.

In 1776, as English colonists wrestled with the tyranny of George III, Dominguez and Escalante left Santa Fe to blaze an overland supply route to Spanish missions in California. Their desire to contact Ute Indians and the uncertainty of the trail westward took them on a swing around the San Juans, over the Uncompahgre Plateau, across Grand Mesa, and finally to the Green River in northeastern Utah. While a series of problems kept the expedition from reaching California, Father Escalante's well-kept diary of the trek provided a valuable description of Colorado's western mountains. Dominguez and Escalante were the first European explorers to travel the length of Colorado's Western Slope and document their achievement.

While the Utes inhabited the high mountains of Colorado, the plains were roamed by tribes of Arapahoe, Kiowa, Cheyenne, and Comanche Indians. In 1779, Comanche raids on New Mexican settlements became so intense that an outraged Spanish governor of New Mexico, Juan Bautista De Anza, marched north from Santa Fe with 600 men to give battle. While previous Spanish explorations had simply crossed Raton Pass and marched across the eastern plains, military strategy dictated that De Anza advance on his enemies by a less conspicuous route.

With the element of surprise in mind, De Anza marched his force up the Rio Grande Valley, through the San Luis Valley, and over Poncha Pass to the headwaters of the Arkansas River. In doing so, De Anza made the first documented penetration of the inner Rockies. Passing under the summits of the Fourteeners of the Sawatch Range, the Governor turned east over Trout Creek Pass, crossed South Park, and descended onto the plains just south of Pikes Peak. If only these adventurers out for gold and glory as well as God and king had known they were riding over what would become the richest gold camp in the world, Cripple Creek!

Once on the plains, De Anza rode south and surprised his adversary, a Comanche chieftain named Cuerno Verde. Cuerno Verde wore a buffalo headdress which boasted two great horns colored with green dye — thus, his Spanish name, meaning "Greenhorn." In a pitched battle just east of Greenhorn Mountain in the Wet Mountains, Cuerno Verde was killed and the Comanche power checked. De Anza returned to New Mexico by crossing Sangre de Cristo Pass just north of the present-day U.S. 160 route across North La Veta Pass, and in so doing, he became the first to circle the Sangre de Cristo Range.

By 1800, Spanish power in the Southwest was rapidly declining and the stage was set for the fledgling United States to flex its muscles of "Manifest Destiny" and discover what lay west of the Mississippi River. In July of 1806, Lieutenant Zebulon Pike, then 27, led an expedition west from St. Louis to explore the southern part of the newly acquired Louisiana Territory and to search for the Red River.

Pike moved up the Arkansas River Valley, and in late November of 1806, he constructed a breastwork of logs at the present site of Pueblo. To the northwest, a great peak towered above the plains. In the first recorded attempt to climb a Colorado Fourteener, Pike and his companions set out for its summit. After two and one-half days, the summit still loomed far away. The explorer abandoned the attempt and promptly noted in his journal that the peak was well over 18,000 feet in elevation and unclimbable in the existing winter conditions. Pike proceeded to entangle himself in the labyrinth of Colorado geography, as well as the intrigue of Spanish politics, during his search for the illusive Red River, but Pikes Peak remains the young explorer's greatest claim to fame.

In the spring of 1820, an Army expedition commanded by Major Stephen H. Long marched west from Council Bluffs to locate the source of another river, the Platte. Long's reports of the Great Plains left the region branded "the Great American Desert" until a later generation of hardy, immigrant farmers proved otherwise.

By June of 1820, Long neared the headwaters of the South Platte and viewed what he first thought to be Pike's "great peak." Only as the expedition crossed the divide separating the Platte and Arkansas valleys, near present day Sedalia, did another great peak loom to the south. Convinced that this second one was Pike's "great peak," Edwin James, the expedition's 23-year-old botanist and physician, set out with a party to attempt its summit. After one and one-half days, James and two companions reached the summit; this was the first documented ascent of a Colorado Fourteener. Their claim must include the word "documented," because there is ample evidence to suggest that Indians and even possibly some wandering Spanish explorers reached the summits of at least several Fourteeners prior to 1820.

James was delighted by the view from the summit and went

into great detail describing the climb in what later became the expedition's official report. Major Long chose to honor James' efforts, which must rank as a pioneering cornerstone in Colorado climbing, by naming the great mountain, "James Peak." Trappers and traders, however, chose to refer to the mountain as "Pikes Peak," and in time James was left to lesser fame. The trappers and traders were kinder to Major Long. The great peak which the expedition first sighted became known as Longs Peak.

Close on the heels of the explorers came the mountain men. These men were a hardy breed who trapped the high streams of the Rockies for beaver, fought Indians (and anyone else in their way), and once a year gathered for a great rendezvous to talk over the season and consume great quantities of "Taos Lightning." That was the name given to the favorite potent drink of the mountain men, one of whom summed up its kick by saying, "It was so strong that no one ever lived long enough to become an addict." The mountain men were so much the "questing type" that it is almost impossible to believe that at least one of them did not venture up some Colorado Fourteener just "to see what was there."

As the fur trade declined, the cry of "Gold!" was raised on the banks of the American River in California, and a tidal wave of prospectors spilled across the continent. The addition of California to the Union in 1850 led some farsighted individuals to dream of a railroad linking East and West. In 1853, four teams of government surveyors crossed the continent to explore possible routes. Captain John W. Gunnison was chosen to lead the exploration of the land between the 38th and 39th parallels.

Gunnison followed the well-established trail of trappers and traders over Sangre de Cristo Pass into the San Luis Valley. The expedition report made particular mention of the spectacular sight which De Anza and Pike had undoubtedly viewed before — the Crestones. Gunnison's route took him past Fort Massachusetts (later Fort Garland), founded in 1852 at the foot of Blanca Peak. Crossing the San Luis Valley, the expedition hauled wagons over Cochetopa Pass, the Utes' "Pass of the Buffalo." By the time he reached the treacherous Black Canyon of the Gunnison River, Captain Gunnison had concluded that any railroad which would dare to battle Colorado's high mountains would require extensive tunneling.

Railroads were fine dreams, but the brewing cauldron of civil war in the East postponed any grand transcontinental schemes. Yet, on the very eve of the Civil War, news came from the Pikes Peak country which was destined to catapult the land of mountains into national prominence. To be sure, the first report was sketchy and the amount of mineral found was small, but the small whisper uttered in May of 1858 at the confluence of Cherry Creek and the South Platte River soon swelled to a hurricane roar of "GOLD!"

By 1859, a new tidal wave of prospectors, speculators, boomers, and get-rich-quick "con" artists poured across the Great Plains with signs of "Pikes Peak or Bust!" For a time, the Front Range dammed the flood of "Fifty-niners" along the eastern Rockies, but within a few years, the lure of new Eldorados in the mountains to the west caused the tidal wave to spill across the high mountain passes into the inner Rockies, thus inexorably entwining the stories of Colorado's people and its mountains.

Giants Above the Plains:
The Front and Mosquito Ranges

To many, the Front Range is the opening scene of Colorado's mountain drama. The farthest east of Colorado's ranges, the Front Range has been the first range to greet many a miner, tourist, and mountaineer from across the endless miles of prairie, and what a fitting introduction it has provided. More than anything else, the Front Range peaks emphasize the awesome height of the Colorado Rockies — soaring up to 8,000 feet above the foothills at their base, a rise no other Colorado range can match.

In the broadest terms, the Front Range applies to the continuous line of mountains which border the Great Plains from the Wyoming border to Canon City, a distance of 180 miles. The Continental Divide passes through the northern part of the range before making a swing westward across the Mosquitos. The South Platte River is the dominant drainage of the eastern slope of the Front Range; the mighty Colorado heads on its western slope north of Grand Lake. The western boundary of the range is not so clearly delineated as the obvious eastern boundary, but is roughly defined by North, Middle, and South parks.

The western border of expansive South Park is formed by the Mosquito Range, which is about 35 miles long and has a 12-mile extension, the Tenmile Range. These two ranges contain five Fourteeners which are of greater interest for their extensive mining history than their mountaineering challenge.

In many ways, the Front Range is the classic example of Colorado's anticlinal ranges. The longest continuous uplift in the state, most of its peaks are composed of Precambrian granite, gneiss, and schist, the overlying Paleozoic sedimentary layers having long since been stripped away. The breaking of the once overlying sedimentary layers is well displayed along the Front Range. Areas of up-sloping sedimentary layers such as the Garden of the Gods and the Flatirons make evident the great forces of the Laramide Orogeny.

After the uplift, intrusive and extrusive igneous activity occurred in many parts of the Front and Mosquito ranges. Many small intrusions were responsible for most of the gold and silver deposits in the Front Range. The largest center of extrusive volcanic activity was in the vicinity of Cripple Creek, now legendary for its mineral wealth.

The mining booms caused the Front and Mosquito ranges to be the first mountain regions of Colorado to be explored and climbed extensively. As the prospectors moved west, they found Ute, Kenosha, Loveland, and Berthoud passes to be gateways through the range and the flat expanse of South Park to be a veritable speedway into the Mosquito Range. Many prospectors continued over Mosquito Pass into Oro City (soon to be overshadowed by Leadville), but some were attracted by the gold placers at the foot of the Mosquitos. As a result, headquarter town Fairplay was established in 1859, and the surrounding Alma Mining District was officially organized two years later.

As the miners searched for the elusive yellow metal in the Front and Mosquito ranges, they also climbed and named many peaks. The naming of the Mosquito Range is attributed to Judge Wilbur F. Stone, who was painfully aware of the abundance of the pests in the rarefied mountain air. Undecided on a name for his new mining company, Judge Stone left the space on the incorporation papers blank and was stumped until a passing mosquito obliged by landing directly on the blank space. Thus, Judge Stone gained the inspiration for the Mosquito Mining Company, and later the name was adopted for the entire range.

As the mining boom spread west, the easier passes through the Front Range were occupied by narrow gauge rails. As the "baby railroads" began to prove that mountain railroading was indeed possible, the standard gauge lines gave it a try. The Colorado Midland climbed Ute Pass in 1886, and the Denver, Northwestern, and Pacific completed its spectacular line over 11,670-foot Rollins Pass, the highest rail pass in North America, in 1907. The culmination of great railroad construction in the Front Range, however, was the completion of the Moffat Tunnel in 1927, which was bored under the Continental Divide for more than six miles beneath James Peak.

Tourism on a small scale was known in the Front Range as

early as the 1860s, but it received real impetus from the extensive rail network and the growth of health spas such as Colorado Springs. As photographic techniques improved, the images of great Front Range sights such as Pikes Peak and Longs Peak were widely circulated throughout the United States as lures to the Centennial State. Consequently, thousands flocked to Colorado and provided revenue never dreamed of in struggling mining towns.

Today, tourism is the most important industry in the Front Range, and no doubt will continue to be, as long as the natural beauty of the area is intelligently protected and preserved. The tremendous population boom the Front Range has experienced in the past three decades makes this protection all the more difficult, but also all the more important.

Longs Peak
14,255 Feet (15th highest)

Longs Peak is undisputedly the monarch of the northern Front Range and one of the outstanding peaks of the entire North American continent. It has gained prominence in the eyes of explorers, settlers, writers, tourists, mountaineers, and technical climbers alike. Longs Peak offers something for virtually everyone, either in its striking beauty or its climbing possibilities, but first and foremost, Longs is a climber's mountain. Even the easiest routes up Longs are classic climbs, and nothing in the Rocky Mountains quite compares with climbs on Longs' mark of individuality — the magnificent 1,675-foot east face, crowned with the sheerest part of all, the 1,000-foot Diamond.

The history of Longs Peak is so rich that any detailed account deserves an entire book. Two such books are Stephen Trimble's *Long's Peak: A Rocky Mountain Chronicle*, which was published in 1984 with some fine color photography, and Paul Nesbit's *Longs Peak — Its Story and a Climbing Guide*, which was the standard guide to the mountain for many years. Also, Bill Bueler's *Roof of the Rockies* devotes a chapter to Longs Peak and vicinity.

While Stephen Long made the first recorded American sighting of the peak which now bears his name in 1820, Longs and its companion, Mount Meeker, had previously been dubbed "Les Deux Orielles" (The Two Ears) by French fur traders who used the pair as a prominent landmark. Longs Peak was the name that stuck, however, and in the early years of settlement, it was one of the foremost unconquered mountaineering challenges in the entire Rocky Mountain region. Its fame spread quickly, even to the extent of becoming the fictional site of a 280-foot telescope in Jules Vernes' *From the Earth to the Moon* in 1866.

Longs' physical dominance made it a natural goal for climbing, and its allure was intensified by the first ascent of the Matterhorn in 1865. Colorado had its own "Matterhorn" in the form of Longs Peak, and reports from climbing parties that the peak could not be scaled only fueled the fire for an ascent. Finally, on August 23, 1868, a party led by the indomitable John Wesley

The upper east face of Longs Peak from the Boulderfield. The cable route once climbed the slope to the right of the east face. The Keyhole lies out of the photograph to the right (west).

Powell and that included newspaperman William Byers reached the summit via the south side after a long approach from Grand Lake. This climb was widely acclaimed as the first ascent of Longs, but the testimony of an old Arapahoe Indian in 1914 indicated that the peak had been climbed previously by one "Old Man Gun," who had trapped eagles on its summit. While the Powell party did not notice an eagle trap on the summit, it may have easily been overlooked in the four-acre expanse, and there is little reason to doubt that the peak was indeed climbed by Indians prior to 1868.

After the first official ascent, two prominent people emerged in the history of Longs Peak — Reverend Elkanah J. Lamb and Enos Mills. Lamb made his first climb of Longs in 1871, and then made the first descent of the east face via a couloir now known as Lambs Slide, appropriately named, because the Reverend quite inadvertently made much of the descent on his seat instead of his feet. In 1878, Lamb became the first regular guide for climbs up Longs, operating out of his lodge to the east of the peak. He charged $5.00 to guide parties up the peak, and once said, "If they would not pay for spiritual guidance, I compelled them to pay for material elevation." By his enthusiasm and his completion of the first trail to the Boulderfield, Lamb contributed immensely to the popularity of climbing Longs; his work was taken over by his son, Carlyle, in 1885. In 1902, the Lambs sold their lodge to Enos Mills, who carried on their tradition of expert guiding in excellent fashion.

Mills was a naturalist of some repute, and his knowledge of the flora and fauna of the area added greatly to a climb of Longs. He constructed the Timberline Cabin in 1908, and made a total of 297 climbs of the peak. Most importantly, Mills' great love for Longs Peak and the surrounding area resulted in a drive to protect the region, which culminated in the creation of Rocky Mountain National Park in 1915.

In 1925, two sets of cables were installed on the north face of the peak to aid in climbing, and until 1973, the majority of climbers ascended by the "Cable Route." In 1927, the Boulderfield Shelter Cabin was erected at the foot of the north face. Many climbers rode on horseback to the cabin and then climbed the peak the next day. The cabin, however, lasted only until 1937, and today very few ride to the Boulderfield before climbing. Climbing Longs has become increasingly popular in recent years, with as many as 4,000 climbers reaching its summit in a single year. Most of these people previously reached the summit via the Cable Route, but on July 20, 1973, the cables were removed, and the circuitous Keyhole Route is now the easiest and most popular route.

While mountaineering has often been thought of as a male sport, Longs was one of the first major United States peaks to be climbed frequently by women. Addie Alexander was the first woman to climb the peak, in 1873, and later that year, Miss Anna Dickinson made her much-heralded climb. Earlier, Miss Dickinson had ascended Pikes, Grays, and Lincoln, mostly by burro, but on Longs she demonstrated her real climbing skill. She accompanied members of the Hayden Survey, and along with them, decided on the naming of nearby Mount Lady Washington and Mount Meeker, for Nathan Meeker, a friend of Anna's who later gained a place in history by being killed by the White River Utes in 1879. Incidentally, Nathan Meeker's son,

Ralph, was along on the climb and was courting Miss Dickinson, but while they reached great heights together on the climb of Longs, they apparently never reached the pinnacle of marriage, much to Ralph's chagrin.

During the month following Miss Dickinson's climb, Miss Isabella Bird, a cultured English author, made the ascent and wrote of it. She was guided by the very uncultured mountain man, Rocky Mountain Jim Nugent, "a man any woman could love, but no sane woman would marry," as Isabella put it. With plenty of "direct aid" from Jim, Miss Bird eventually did make the summit, and then wrote of her experiences in *A Lady's Life in the Rocky Mountains*, which was great publicity for the Longs Peak area and is still entertaining reading.

Technical climbing on Longs did not come into vogue until the 1920s. While the great east face had been descended by Lamb in 1871, and by Mills in 1903, that side was not climbed until Werner Zimmerman did it in 1919. A more direct and now classic route was pioneered by James Alexander in 1922. After these ice-breaking ascents, climbs of Longs' east face read like a list of climbing all-stars. Carl Blaurock, the Stettner brothers, Tom Hornbein, and Layton Kor are just a few of the many climbers who have pioneered new routes on Longs.

While many new routes were found on the east face of the peak, the ultimate technical climb, the ascent of the spectacular, 1,000-foot sheer Diamond Face, was not accomplished until 1960, due in part to National Park climbing restrictions before that year. In the summer of 1960, the restrictions were lifted, and California climbers David Rearick and Robert Kamps gained the right to begin an assault on the Diamond on August 1. After two days of difficult rock and aid climbing with obviously incredible exposure, the two reached the summit of Longs on the afternoon of August 3. Since this milestone in Longs Peak climbing history, a number of other climbs of the Diamond have been made, including the first winter ascent in 1967 by Layton Kor and Wayne Goss. The great east face of Longs will unquestionably continue to challenge climbers for generations to come, and, as Robert Ormes has stated, Longs peak will continue to boast "the nation's greatest concentration of high country rock routes."

Due to the extreme popularity of Longs (it is estimated that nearly 100,000 have climbed it), it is inevitable that a number of fatalities have occurred. From 1884 to 1972, 26 fatalities were reported, the causes ranging from gunshot wounds to falls to lightning. The most publicized of these fatalities was the Agnes Vaille tragedy which followed the first successful winter ascent of the east face by Miss Vaille and Walter Keiner in 1925. On the descent near the Boulderfield, she collapsed from exhaustion; Keiner went for help, but she froze to death. To add further sadness, Herbert Sortland, a member of the rescue party, became lost, and he also died. While such fatalities as this are often highly publicized, it must be remembered that 26 fatalities out of nearly 100,000 ascents is an extremely small percentage and that Longs has been safely climbed by five-year-olds, an eighty-five-year-old, people on crutches, and a six-piece band.

While Longs Peak is a worthy goal in itself, perhaps it achieved its greatest worth by providing training for four members of the 1963 American Everest Expedition. Allen Auten, Barry Bishop, Dick Pownall, and Thomas Hornbein all attributed climbs of Longs as important in their climbing development. Of these, Bishop and Hornbein reached the summit of Everest and thus Longs Peak gained the prestige of playing a part in the conquest of another great peak more than twice its height.

In 1974, Longs achieved literary fame as an important geographic landmark in James Michener's classic novel, *Centennial.* In *Centennial,* Michener referred to Longs as the peak upon which a huge stone beaver appears to be climbing upward. Indeed, if one looks closely, and with imagination, a beaver does appear etched against the skyline, just to the south of the Diamond Face — just one more unique feature of the incomparable personality of Longs Peak.

T H E   R O U T E S

Keyhole Route

Since the removal of the cables, the standard route available to the nontechnical climber is the Keyhole route. Drive south from Estes Park ten miles on Colorado 7, and turn off for one mile west to the Longs Peak Campground and Ranger Station, at 9,400 feet. From here, an excellent trail leads six miles to the Boulderfield. Hop over the abundant boulders for one mile to the prominent Keyhole at the southwest corner of the Boulder-

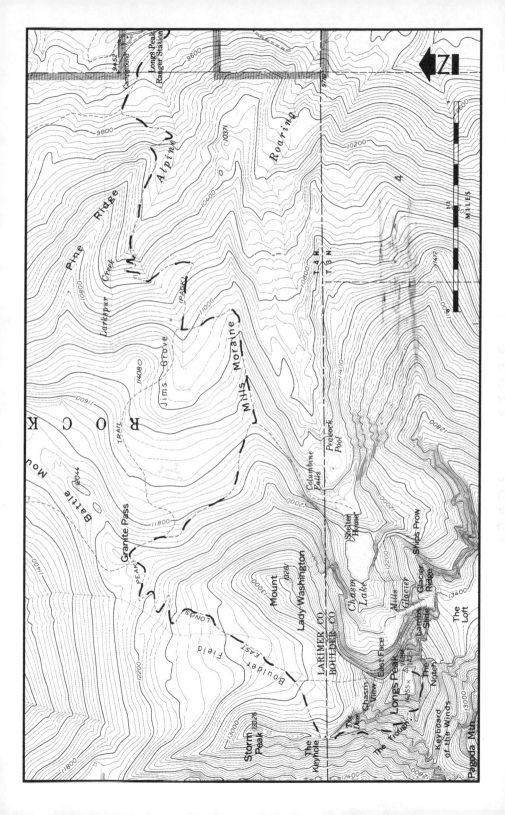

field. Just to the left of the Keyhole lies the Agnes Vaille Shelter Cabin, which shelters more snow than anything. Once through the Keyhole (13,100 feet) the route is marked by red and yellow paint spots, which lead over the Ledges and into the broad couloir known as "the Trough." It is then 600 steep feet up the snow and/or talus of the Trough to a notch at the top of it.

At the notch, the still-marked route swings to the south side of the peak, and immediately crosses the most spectacular part of the climb, the Narrows ledges. The Narrows are fairly exposed, but they are broad enough to be crossed easily if there is no snow. *If there is snow*, which is a possibility until well into July, an ice axe is a necessity for a safe climb of the Ledges, the Trough, the Narrows, and the Homestretch. The Narrows lead to the bottom of the Homestretch, a short couloir leading directly to the summit. Descend via the same route. Do not underestimate Longs. It is a long climb and if it is snowy or icy, the Keyhole route requires an ice axe and the ability to use it correctly. Note: The National Park Service permits backcountry camping only in designated areas. Permits are required and reservations well in advance are strongly recommended for the peak summer season. The main Rocky Mountain National Park information number is (303) 586-2371.

Longs Peak Ranger Station to Summit: 8 miles, 4,800 feet.

▲

Mount Evans
14,264 feet (14th highest)

Mount Bierstadt
14,060 feet (38th highest)

Dominating the Front Range skyline to the west of Denver is the sprawling massif of Mount Evans. Connected to Mount Evans with the forbidding Sawtooth Ridge is Mount Bierstadt, lying one and one-half miles west of Evans and therefore not visible from Denver. The Evans massif figured as a prominent landmark early in Colorado history, and during the gold rush of the 1860s was known simply as the Chicago Mountains; as one might expect, it was named by a group of 1859 miners who hailed from the Windy City.

Evans and Bierstadt are the only two Colorado Fourteeners whose histories are tied closely with the life of a painter. Albert Bierstadt is perhaps the best known painter of great Western scenes in the 1860s and '70s, and it is fitting that a Colorado Fourteener bears his name. Bierstadt made his first trip west in 1858, when he journeyed to famed South Pass in Wyoming. On that trip, he was inspired to paint *Morning in the Rocky Mountains* and *Rocky Mountains — Landers Peak*, the latter of which measures six feet by ten feet, a typical size for Bierstadt's work.

In 1863, Bierstadt began his second trip west and, with William Byers, visited the Chicago Mountains. Bierstadt climbed some of the peaks of this "range" and may well have made the first ascents of both Mount Evans and Mount Bierstadt, although there was some mining activity not far from Mount Bierstadt at that time. While camped at the Chicago Lakes, north of Mount Evans, Bierstadt was impressed by a large storm cloud playing about the summit of Mount Evans (which he had christened Mount Rosalie for his wife). Afterward, in 1866, he painted *Storm in the Rocky Mountains*, which featured this scene. After the 1863 trip, Bierstadt made four additional trips west and continued

Mount Evans from the north across the Chicago Lakes Basin. Summit Lake lies beneath the snowfield beyond the headwall of the basin. *Colorado Historical Society.*

producing huge, sensational, Western paintings, including a classic one of Longs Peak, which now hangs in the Denver Public Library's Western History Room.

While Albert Bierstadt would have loved having Mount Rosalie retained as a name for the highest peak of the Chicago Mountains, it was not. In 1870, at a celebration in Greeley, it was suggested that Mount Rosalie be renamed "Mount Evans," in honor of Colorado's second territorial governor who served from 1862 to 1865. John Evans had no spectacular achievements on the political front, but after his retirement from the political scene, he promoted the building of the Denver Pacific Railroad and the Denver, South Park and Pacific. He also donated the property upon which the University of Denver was eventually built, and he was one of the original supporters of the Colorado State Historical Society. The name change was popularly supported, and Mount Rosalie was renamed "Mount Evans" by a Colorado legislature resolution on March 5, 1895, coinciding with Evans' 81st birthday. The name "Rosalie" was then applied

Mount Bierstadt (right) and the Sawtooth with the tip of Mount Evans visible from Guanella Pass with the infamous willows in the foreground.

to a 13,575-foot peak southeast of Mount Evans. Mount Bierstadt was officially named in 1914, as proposed by Ellsworth Bethel.

While not as accessible as Pikes Peak during the first two decades of the twentieth century, Evans and Bierstadt were relatively popular with climbers. One climber who frequented Mount Evans was Albert R. Ellingwood (see La Plata Peak), who climbed Mount Evans on snowshoes in March of 1916. Ellingwood also probably made the first ascent of Evans' 600-foot north face in 1922, just as safe technical climbing was being introduced in the United States. Mount Bierstadt also saw some climbing at this time, and while not offering the challenges of technical climbs, it may have been ski-climbed for the first time in 1934. The date of the first traverse of the ragged Sawtooth Ridge between Evans and Bierstadt is not known, but it is likely that it also occurred in the 1920s or 1930s.

In the 1930s, a crude road was constructed to the summit of Evans, and thus it became the second and last (hopefully!) Colorado Fourteener on which one could drive to the summit.

In 1939, the road was improved and was widely hailed as the highest automobile road in the world. In 1941, the original summit house was constructed, and flocks of tourists began invading the mountain. In addition, scientists discovered the summit of Evans to be a convenient location for high-altitude studies, and the University of Denver built its Cosmic Ray Research Laboratory there in 1936. A wide variety of experiments have been conducted there and in July of 1973, a 4-ton, 24-inch reflector telescope was installed, becoming the highest fixed astronomical telescope in the world. Mount Evans is an ideal site for an observatory because of its accessibility and the dryness of the Colorado air at 14,000 feet, which makes for ideal viewing conditions.

In the summer months, when the paved road is open to the summit, Mount Evans swarms with people desiring to avoid the heat and congestion of the city. As a result, climbing accidents have become more frequent on the peak. In late August and early September of 1976, two fatalities occurred on Evans within a two-week period. The first victim was Brian Driscoll, 28, who attempted to descend from the summit via the treacherous snow and ice couloirs of the north face. He slipped, slid out of control for 600 feet, and was fatally injured on the rocks below. Then, in early September, Thomas R. Gibbons, 18, also lost his footing on the snow and fell about 400 feet. Despite first aid given by fishermen, he died before a rescue helicopter could reach him. Even Colorado's most popular and easiest peaks can be deadly if one is ill-equipped and inexperienced — know your abilities!

THE ROUTES

Mount Evans, Summit Lake

While Mount Evans can be climbed in very short order and with only about 30 feet of elevation gain from the parking lot on top, a longer climb with an expansive view of the plains can be made from Summit Lake (12,830 feet). From Idaho Springs, drive 24 miles up the Mount Evans road, or drive 31 miles from Bergen Park, which connects with the Mount Evans road at mile 14, and park at Summit Lake.

The summit of Evans is clearly visible one-half mile south of this point, and reaching it involves a steep but not difficult climb which finishes on large rocks. Be certain to avoid the cliffs

and the treacherous snow and ice couloirs to the west (right) of this route. The summit house has been closed in recent years due to a fire, so pack your own coffee.

Summit Lake to Mount Evans: ½ mile; 1,400 feet.

Mount Evans, Chicago Lakes

From Echo Lake Lodge (10,650), walk west on the south side of the lake on one of several trails to a sandy area under overhead lines where several trails criss-cross at the southwest corner of the lake. The trail to Chicago Lakes crosses over the ridge to the west near some boulders and begins a gradual descent into the Chicago Creek drainage. The trail crosses Chicago Creek to the west, just south of private property at Camp Shwayder, follows the road to the Idaho Springs reservoir, and then climbs south through a major burn. From the upper lake, climb south to Summit Lake and the route described above. Quite frankly, the best part of this route is the lakes and some wonderful crags on the western side. Those desiring a longer climb of Evans are probably better served by climbing Evans from the west via some combination of the routes described below.

Echo Lake to Mount Evans: 6 miles; 4,000 feet.

Mount Bierstadt, Guanella Pass

From Georgetown, drive south up the Guanella Pass road for ten miles to the immediate vicinity of the pass (11,669). The rounded summit of Bierstadt appears to the east along with the jagged Sawtooth in impressive relief against the sky. Guanella Pass may also be approached from the south, ten miles from Grant on U.S. 285. From the pass, one of the classic Colorado climbing obstacles is confronted — the infamous Guanella Pass willows! Once there were only rumors of a trail through the three- to five-foot high vegetation between the road and the base of the peak. Small children and climbers under five-ten often roped up. In recent years, however, a trail has become increasingly clear, although it is most obvious from the peak side — a fact that does little to soothe those early morning encounters with dew in the willow patch. Once across the willows, the climb two miles east to the summit up a pleasant grassy ridge is easily accomplished. Bierstadt makes a great ski climb if the snow is well-packed over the willows and avalanche danger is low.

Guanella Pass to Mount Bierstadt: 3 miles; 2,500 feet.

Evans and Bierstadt, The Sawtooth Ridge

One of Colorado's most impressive ridges is the Sawtooth that connects Evans and Bierstadt. Despite its fearsome look, it is a relatively moderate scramble if it is free of ice and snow. From the summit of Evans, follow the west ridge northwest then southwest one mile to the tip of the prominent Sawtooth. From this approach, the Sawtooth drops away abruptly. Just when you are certain a rapell is necessary, continue west across the high point and down about 100 feet. A prominent series of welcome ledges leads down the west side of the tooth to the bottom of the cliff. From the Sawtooth's base a series of ups and downs with good handholds and some exposure on the west side leads south a half-mile to Bierstadt's summit. Obstacles are best skirted on the east side of the ridge. The route is a good warmup for other ridges, such as Wilson-El Diente and Little Bear-Blanca.

Evans summit to Bierstadt summit: 2 miles, 800 feet.

▲

Grays Peak
14,270 feet (9th highest)

Torreys Peak
14,267 feet (11th highest)

During the 1870s and 1880s, when reference was made to Colorado's most famous mountains, it was not the famous peaks of Pike and Long which were mentioned, but rather two summits named after two of America's most noted botanists. Asa Gray and John Torrey first achieved fame in 1838, by publishing the first part of their monumental *Flora of North America*. Reference to "Torrey and Gray" in botanical circles soon became as widely accepted as reference to "Ormes" among Colorado climbers.

In 1861, Charles C. Parry, a student and co-worker of Torrey and Gray, who was destined to become an eminent botanist in his own right, climbed the higher peaks of the Front Range and took altitude readings. The prominent "Twin Peaks" or "Ant Hills," as Indians called them, Parry named after his colleagues, Torrey and Gray. A lesser peak, just to the north, he named after botanist George Engelmann.

Four years later, in the summer of 1865, three roaring prospectors, Richard Irwin, John Baker, and Fletcher Kelso, stormed into the large valley north of the peaks hunting the ever-elusive glimmer of gold and silver. Locally, Torreys Peak became known as Irwins Peak, while Baker gave his name to the little town of Bakerville, and Kelso replaced Engelmann's name with his own on Kelso Mountain. Always a promoter, Dick Irwin soon had a horse trail leading up Grays Peak, the easier of the twin peaks, and was encouraging tourists to take in the view.

The names of Torreys, Grays, and Irwins Peak changed back and forth until 1872, when visits by Parry, Gray, and Torrey to the peaks helped to establish Grays as the eastern summit and Torreys as the western summit. Gray made a climb of Grays Peak with Parry in July of 1872; Torrey visited Georgetown in Au-

Grays Peak (left) and Torreys Peak (right) from the slopes of McClellan Mountain above the Stevens mine.

gust and was content with the fact that his daughter reached its summit.

Dick Irwin moved on to give his name to a boom-town silver camp in the Gunnison country in 1879, and for 25 years continued to follow the lure of the mining frontier, eventually finding his way to Nome, Alaska, in 1901. The tourist business he had first encouraged on Grays and Torreys, however, reached boom proportions during the 1870s and 1880s. Tourists came from all over the country, and accounts of their climbs made national news. Published accounts appeared in such premiere magazines of the day as *Atlantic Monthly, Overland Monthly, Appleton's Journal, Scribner's,* and the *Appalachia Journal.*

By 1884, when the Colorado Central Railroad had completed the famous Georgetown Loop and passengers could ride in comfort to Silver Plume, Grays and Torreys were musts for tourists bent on seeing Colorado. The ascents were described as "an easy day for a lady," providing, of course, that one rode horseback to the top, as most did!

Despite their reputations on the tourist circuit, Grays and

Torreys were very much mining mountains. In the late 1800s, when Georgetown and the Clear Creek Valley were one of the key mining regions of the state, claims were staked and major properties developed in the high valleys surrounding Grays and Torreys. Of particular note were the Waldorf and Santiago mines on McClellan Mountain to the east and the National Treasure and Peruvian mines in Horseshoe Basin to the south. Perhaps the most famous, however, was the Stevens Mine in Stevens Gulch northeast of the peaks, where Dick Irwin and his cronies first prospected in 1865. Several decaying buildings and a large tailings dump remain today as testaments to a once booming operation which combed the innards of McClellan Mountain with a series of tunnels and shafts.

T H E   R O U T E S

Stevens Gulch

From Georgetown, once the mining metropolis of the Clear Creek Valley, drive west on I-70 six miles to the Bakerville (once called Graymont) exit. Enroute, one passes the Georgetown Loop Historic Mining Area, a Colorado Historical Society project, featuring the restored Georgetown Loop of the old Georgetown, Breckenridge & Leadville Railway. At Bakerville (what little there is left of it), a dirt road climbs south up Stevens Gulch for three miles almost to the Stevens Mine. One mile from Bakerville, the road forks as Kelso Mountain looms ahead. Take the left-hand (east) fork past a delightfully photogenic old millhouse. The road is passable in cars if it is dry, and it makes a fine cross-country ski approach for winter ascents, if one can avoid the ski-doos which frequent the valley. From just below the Stevens Mine, a trail crosses the creek west (11,300 feet) and winds southwest two miles into the large cirque between Grays and Torreys. From here, the standard old horse trail (with some variations) climbs a circuitous one and one-half miles to the summit of Grays. Torreys is one-half mile north with a 500-foot drop.

Stevens Mine to Grays and Torreys: 4 miles; 3,500 feet.

Torreys, North Ridge

The mountaineer will definitely enjoy foregoing the trail for the pleasure of Torreys' north ridge. From the large cirque climb

west to the low point of the Torreys-Kelso saddle just south of an old cabin. The ridge has several airy places — the most thrilling one is several hundred feet below the summit where one looks left (east) into the prominent east-face couloir and right off the north face — it requires some bouldering but serves as a good introduction to ridge-running on Colorado's peaks. After the ridge, the waltz south to Grays and down the trail (good glissades are hard to find), is permissable without robbing one of a feeling of having done a good day's work. The proximity to Denver and the easy nature of the main trail make the "GT" a natural for beginner and family climbs. The high basin also offers campsites studded with wildflowers for those wishing to make an "overnighter" out of it.

The particularly energetic may wish to explore an alternate route to the peaks from the Peru Creek drainage, either Chihuahua Gulch or Horseshoe Basin, to the south which is reached from old U.S. 6 east of Dillon.

▲

Pikes Peak

14,110 feet (31st highest)

Pikes Peak requires no introduction, for even before the name "Colorado" was applied to the territory encompassing the highest part of the Rockies, Pikes Peak was almost a household word. Its massive, rounded prominence from the Great Plains made its fame inevitable, and when gold was discovered well to the north in 1858, the subsequent rush became known as the "Pikes Peak Gold Rush," as if the mountain held dominion from New Mexico to the high plains of Wyoming. Since that time, Pikes Peak has developed a unique history revolving around tourism; to many Americans, it remains the grandest symbol of the Colorado Rockies.

After Zebulon Pike's valiant but unsuccessful attempt to scale the peak in 1806, no further attempts were made until 1820, when the summit was attained by three members of Stephen Long's expedition. The leader of the summit party was Dr. Edwin James, a prominent botanist. On July 13, 1820, he and two others set out for the base of the great peak, prudently allowing three days for the climb. They reached the eastern foot of the mountain the first day, passing a group of large hot springs which, unknown to them, would one day become the nationally famous Manitou Springs. That evening, they camped below timberline, but the next day they entered the magical world above the trees for the first time. The alpine tundra was an unexplored world for James, and he delighted in collecting and taking notes on the abundant alpine flowers of the peak's upper slopes.

On the afternoon of July 14, Edwin James and his two companions stood on the summit of the great peak — the first recorded ascent of a United States Fourteener. James recorded a detailed description of the far-reaching vista, and after an hour of soaking up the view, the trio descended to a makeshift camp for the night. The following morning, they descended to their base camp, only to find that their smoldering campfire had set several acres of the surrounding forest on fire! Incapable of battling the blaze themselves, they hastily made their way back

Pikes Peak from the northeast; the Barr Trail climbs the gentle eastern flanks, while the western route gains the northwest ridge near the first prominent hump from the right. *Colorado Historical Society.*

to the main body of Long's expedition, leaving the fire to burn itself out.

As a result of James' feat, Major Long christened the great mountain "James Peak." A great confusion of names resulted in subsequent years, however. "Pikes Peak" was more commonly used on an informal basis. Finally, in 1843, the issue was settled when explorer John Fremont used the name Pikes Peak on one of his maps. Since then, James' name has been given to a prominent thirteener in the vicinity of Berthoud Pass.

In the years that followed, it was natural that Pikes would become an enticing climb, as it was the first Fourteener to greet many flatlanders as they traveled west. A crude trail was constructed to the summit in the 1850s, and in 1858, Julia A. Holmes reached the summit, becoming the first woman to scale a North American Fourteener. Mrs. Holmes later went on to become a driving force in women's suffrage, and in later mountaineering exploits, she showed herself equal to men in climbing ability. Pikes became quite a popular goal for many women, and in

1893, Katherine Lee Bates was inspired to write the words to her immortal "America the Beautiful" from its summit.

In 1871, the Pikes Peak area became the resort center of the Rockies with the founding of Colorado Springs by William Jackson Palmer. His newly completed Denver and Rio Grande Railway brought many visitors to "Little London" to relax and enjoy the magnificent view of Pikes Peak. In 1874, the boiling springs which James had seen were commercially developed, and Manitou Springs grew rapidly as an important resort and health center. A massive advertising campaign promoted the Pikes Peak region as the health capital of the United States, which, if not heaven itself, was close enough to heaven to make a 1,000-or-2,000-mile-trip worthwhile.

Of course, Pikes Peak was at the heart of all of this publicity, and better trails to its summit were constructed in the 1870s. The most popular trail was and is the Barr Trail, which starts directly from Manitou Springs and climbs 7,500 feet and 12 miles to the summit, more of an elevation gain than any other Colorado Fourteener. Improved access to the summit of Pikes did not stop with better trails, however. For those who did not want to climb the peak, but preferred to sit all the way to the top, a carriage road was constructed in 1889. A scant one year later, the ultimate means of transportation comfort of the day reached the summit of Pikes via an easterly and southerly approach — the railroad.

The Manitou and Pikes Peak Cog Railway climbs 8.9 miles from Manitou Springs to the summit on a 25 percent grade. At that time, it was the highest railroad in the world, and today is still the highest standard-gauge line in the world, as some narrow-gauge railroads in the Andes reach in excess of 15,000 feet. A small resort flourished for a short while at Halfway House Station on the railroad, but this lasted only until 1926. As if the railroad were not enough, the first automobile reached the summit of Pikes in 1901 via the crude carriage road.

Pikes Peak suffered its final humiliation when the old carriage road was converted into an automobile road in 1915. The major promoter of this construction was Spencer Penrose, a Harvard graduate who lived in Colorado Springs. Penrose built the road at a cost of a quarter of a million dollars, and to help offset this cost, he organized the first Pikes Peak Hill Climb the following year. Twenty racers entered the first race, which was won by Rea

Lentz in an eight-cylinder Romano. The tradition has continued, and today the Pikes Peak Hill Climb is one of the more unusual auto races in the United States. Penrose, meanwhile, did not stop his promotions with this race. In 1918, he put the icing on the cake of all his promotions with the completion of the two-million-dollar Broadmoor, the plushest of all Colorado's resorts, at the foot of Cheyenne Mountain.

Pikes Peak and the surrounding region remain a major recreation and vacation area today. The north side of the peak has attracted winter recreation in the form of a small ski area, and in the summer, the health theme is further promoted with the annual foot race up the Barr Trail. Four divisions are represented, and the race is one of the most grueling in the nation. Another special event was initiated in 1921 — the New Year's climb of the peak and associated fireworks from the summit. It is carried out annually by the Colorado Springs AdAmAn Club.

Each year, in the summer months when the road is open all the way to the top, more than 250,000 people drive to the summit, and perhaps then enjoy a cup of coffee in the summit house while leisurely soaking in the unparalleled view. While it is in some ways objectionable to the mountaineer to have a road to the summit of what was once solely a climber's peak, perhaps it is justifiable that the legendary view from the summit of this legendary mountain is available to all Americans.

T H E   R O U T E S

The Barr Trail

This is the classic route up Pikes Peak, but because of its length and 7,500-foot elevation gain, it can be quite rugged as a one-day climb even if one is superbly conditioned. For a two-day climb, the best camping site is at Barr's Camp, at 9,800 feet. In Manitou Springs, follow Ruxton Avenue west to the trailhead parking area just beyond the Pikes Peak Cog Railroad depot. The trail leaves from the parking lot and then it is "merely" a trail climb to the summit, 12 incredible miles distant.

Parking area to Summit: 12 miles; 7,500 feet.

The Crags Campground, North Ridge

While the Barr Trail is the classic route up Pikes and the

most popular, a shorter route but one with a tremendous view is available from an approach from the west. From Divide, 25 miles west of Colorado Springs on U.S. 24, turn south on Colorado 67 four miles to a left (east) turnoff at sign reading "Rocky Mountain Camp." Drive east on this road past the Mennonite Rocky Mountain Camp one and one-half miles up, for a total of three miles to The Crags Campground. Park here at 10,000 feet, and locate the signed trailhead to the Crags themselves at the east end of the campground. After hiking only about 200 yards up this trail, the critical part of the route is encountered. At about this point, the stream to the south of the trail, Fourmile Creek, forks, with an east-northeast branch, and an east-southeast branch. By crossing the former, the closest one, a very old logging road, actually more of a trail here, will be found between the forks very near their confluence, which follows the east-southeast branch. It is important that this road is found, for missing it will lead you into the wrong drainage. (If you follow the Crags Trail into a small meadow flanked on the left by a large granite slab, you have gone too far; return and search out the stream junction.)

Once on the rocky old logging road, hike up it, taking a left at the one junction not far from its start. From here, the old road parallels the stream up the valley for one and one-half miles, where an old logged-out slope with many three-foot-high stumps appears directly ahead. At the foot of this area, the road swings north. After making this turn, watch for a trail heading to the right through the logged-out area within a quarter-mile of the turn. If this trail cannot be found, merely angle upslope east-south-east through this area, heading for the low saddle in the grassy ridge at the head of the drainage, one mile distant. If the trail is found, it continues to timberline, and from there it is an easy climb to the 12,700-foot saddle. The saddle brings you in full view of the summit of Pikes and the toll road. Follow the spur road which appears on the east side of the saddle to the main road. Cross the main road (watch for traffic!) and hike 50 to 100 feet above and paralleling the highway, keeping to the left wherever possible. This serves two purposes. First, it keeps you from being scrutinized too closely by every tourist who drives by, and second, it keeps you from being stopped by the local patrol who frown on people hiking on the road. Hike along the flats for about two miles to the base of the summit cone. From here, it is about 600 more feet in elevation up the broken rocks on the north side of the summit cone. Descend via the same route.

The Crags Campground to Summit: 7 miles; 4,100 feet.

▲

Quandary Peak

14,265 feet (13th highest)

Quandary Peak reportedly gets its name from a group of miners who were in a quandary to identify a mineral specimen on its slopes. Indeed, however, the very fact that the peak was referred to as McCullough's Peak, Ute Peak, and Hoosier Peak may have left just about everyone in a quandary as to its name.

While fur traders and trappers from South Park and the drainage of the South Platte River surely viewed the peak, the "Pathfinder of the West" himself, John C. Fremont, got the first recorded close-up of the peak on June 22, 1844, when his second expedition to the Rockies crossed yet-unnamed Hoosier Pass from the drainage of the Blue River to the headwaters of the South Platte. Fremont's expedition solved a perplexing riddle of central Colorado geography by discovering the relationship of the Gore Range, the Blue Valley, and South Park to the headwaters of the Arkansas River.

As the mining rush of 1859 spilled beyond the Front Range, a homesick band of Indiana prospectors crossed the pass and, although it was sometimes called Ute Pass, christened it Hoosier Pass. The riddle of names was finally solved in the Hayden Atlas, which correctly labeled the pass, "Hoosier," and the mountain, "Quandary."

In June of 1861, a party of eight wagons pioneered the first wheeled crossing of Hoosier Pass going from Breckenridge to Fairplay. The Mosquito Range soon felt the full brunt of the mining rush. Claims were staked on Quandary Peak and in the basin of the Blue Lakes and Monte Cristo Creek. Quandary City, two miles southeast of the peak, sprang up as a collection of tents and hastily constructed cabins.

THE ROUTES

Monte Cristo Creek

Quandary is a fine family climb as well as an easily accessible winter ascent. On the north side of Hoosier Pass on Colorado

Quandary Peak looking north across North Star Peak from Mount Lincoln, showing the prominent descent couloir from the summit. *Craig F. Koontz.*

9, eight miles south of Breckenridge or fourteen miles north of Fairplay, on a prominent curve, a road leads west along Monte Cristo Creek to Monte Cristo Reservoir. Quandary is easily recognizable from the summit of Hoosier Pass as the long-ridged mountain to the northwest. The long east ridge may be reached from any point along the Monte Cristo road. The most gentle approach climbs an old logging road a half-mile west of Colorado 9 to the broad ridge and then west two and one-half miles to the summit. The farther west one goes on the Monte Cristo road, the steeper the summit climb becomes. From the summit, a perfect couloir descends the south face, and in ideal spring conditions, it will deposit one squarely at the Monte Cristo Reservoir dam after five minutes and one of the best glissades in the state. Just climb down several hundred feet south from the summit, sit down, and go for it! Ice axes are required.

Colorado 9 to Summit: 3 miles, 3,500 feet.

From the summit of Quandary, rugged Pacific Peak (13,950

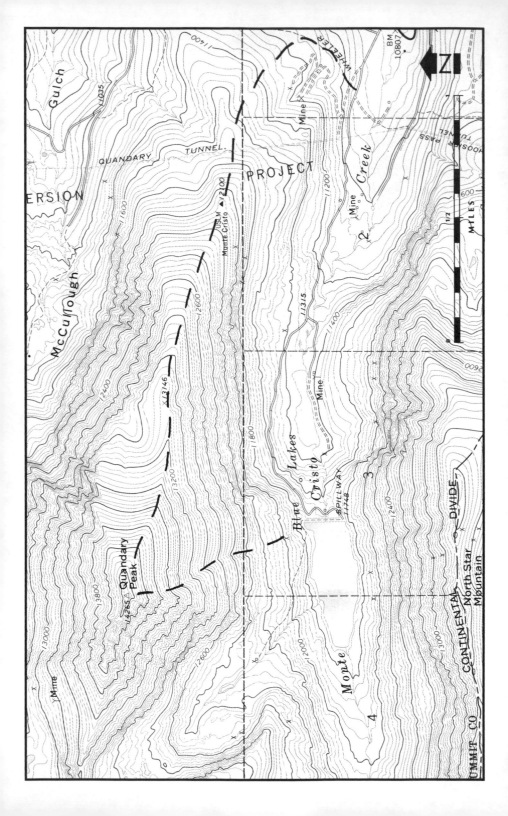

feet) is a fine view to the northwest. The Monte Cristo Valley also offers an approach to Fletcher Mountain (13,955 feet) to the west, as well as the spectacle of mine buildings clinging to the north slope of North Star to the south like sparrows to telephone lines in a gale.

▲

Mount Lincoln
14,286 feet (8th highest)

Mount Democrat
14,148 feet (29th highest)

Mount Bross
14,172 feet (22th highest)

If Longs Peak is known as a climber's mountain and Pikes Peak as a tourist's mountain, then history must justly accord Mount Lincoln the title of a miner's mountain. From the first flow of prospectors into the Mosquito Range in the early 1860s to the present, literally every inch of Mount Lincoln and its neighbors from summit cairns to valleys below has felt the ring of miners' picks. All three summits were undoubtedly reached by prospectors and quite possibly by Indians before them.

In June of 1861, Wilbur F. Stone, whose pondering on a mining company name spawned the name "Mosquito" and who later helped to draft Colorado's constitution, ascended the highest peak above Hoosier Pass. After taking thermometer tests, he promptly pronounced it to be over 17,000 feet and returned to the mining camp of Montgomery at the mountain's eastern base to describe the peak's wonders and give it a name. In the best of grand legend, the story is told that after a number of names were suggested, the name of the recently elected President was raised by the crowd as if in one voice, and Mount Lincoln it became.

Stone's estimate, perpetuated by boastful miners, of Lincoln's elevation influenced a number of later atypically high readings. Undoubtedly, casual observers were fooled into believing that Lincoln towered 6,000 to 7,000 feet above the broad expanse of South Park much like the Front Range does above the plains.

Mount Bross (left) and Mount Lincoln (right) looking west from Hoosier Pass across Montgomery Reservoir.

South Park, however, is already a lofty 10,000 feet. As late as 1867, George Pine recounted in his travelogue, *Beyond the West*, that the peak was well above 15,000 feet. In style typical of the romantic adventure of the day, Pine wrote a vivid description of Lincoln rising above Montgomery City and concluded, "I never realized such poverty of language as when I stood upon that commanding peak."

Lincoln's two neighbors only broaden the massive appearance of Lincoln. Mount Bross, whose greatest claim to fame may be the fact that it boasts the broadest, roundest summit of the Fifty-Four, was named for William Bross, who owned mining property near Alma. Bross owed his celebrity status largely to the fact that he served as lieutenant governor of Illinois from 1865 to 1869 and claimed Colorado mining legend "Commodore" Steven Decatur as his long-lost brother, much to the Commodore's denial. Bross made an ascent of Lincoln with Father John Dyer, the famed "Snowshoe Itinerant," in 1876, and was so enthusiastic about the view that local miners began referring to Lincoln's south peak as Mount Bross.

Mount Democrat looking west from the slopes of Mount Bross.
Lyndon J. Lampert.

Mount Democrat bore the name of "Buckskin" in the Hayden Atlas, named after the rip-roaring Buckskin Joe mining camp northwest of Fairplay. The name "Democrat" does not appear to be documented until the Land Office Survey of 1883. As elsewhere, the great influx of miners in the Mosquitos left countless stories, many bordering on legend, if not outright fiction. By one account, however, the name "Democrat" came from a group of rebellious southerners during the Civil War who of course were strongly opposed to Abraham Lincoln.

Although in rapidly deteriorating condition, a number of mining buildings still dot the slopes of the three peaks, reminders of hard-rock miners working claims with names such as Dora, Addie, Crown, Reliance, Snowbird, Moscow, Russia, Alhambra, Balconia, and the Mary, which included the very summit of Mount Bross. Remnants of two of Bross' largest mines, the Dolly Varden and the Moose, still stand near 13,000 feet on the peak's northeast flank. Both silver producers, the mines produced $3,000,000 by 1878. The Russia Mine, located several hundred feet southeast of Lincoln's summit, was one of the largest operations on that peak and boasted silver ore worth up to $500 per ton. The Kentucky Belle was the premiere operation between Democrat and Bross in the valley above Kite Lake and made its reputation on gold ore assaying out to almost $900 per ton on choice loads.

Encircling the eastern slopes of Lincoln and Bross, from Hoosier Pass to Fairplay, there was a string of mining towns, Montgomery, Quartzville, Buckskin Joe, Dudleyville, Mosquito, Park City, and Alma. Only Alma survives. Most of the towns were built to serve a particular group of mines. When the mines ceased operations or declined in production, the towns quickly died. Quartzville, for example, served the rich Moose and Dolly Varden claims on Bross. Today, only a few crumbling buildings remain in the shallow bowl at the mouth of the gulch between Lincoln and Bross as reminders of its existence.

T H E   R O U T E S

Although rated as easy climbs technically, Lincoln, Democrat, and Bross all in one day for beginners or the ill-conditioned can be an exhausting experience. Two main approach routes are recommended for all or any combination of the three.

Kite Lake

You may want to have a delicious breakfast at the world-famous Fairplay Hotel before you drive seven miles northwest on Colorado 9 to Alma, then seven miles northwest up Buckskin Gulch on Park County 10 to Kite Lake (12,000 feet). The road is passable in cars to a steep hill just below the lake. From the lake, Democrat is a one-mile climb northwest via the Cameron-Democrat saddle and Democrat's northeast ridge. At least one group chose to ascend via the jagged south ridge of Democrat and promptly christened the ridge with a name which described it as being a pain to the posterior section of the anatomy. From Democrat, Cameron is one and one-half miles east after an agonizing drop of 750 feet, the greatest drop of the three saddles. From Cameron, Lincoln is an easy stroll northeast along a ridge which stays above 14,000 feet. Then it's back to Cameron and one mile southeast to big, broad Bross whose summit cairn does stand out slightly in the midst of its spacious summit. The Came-

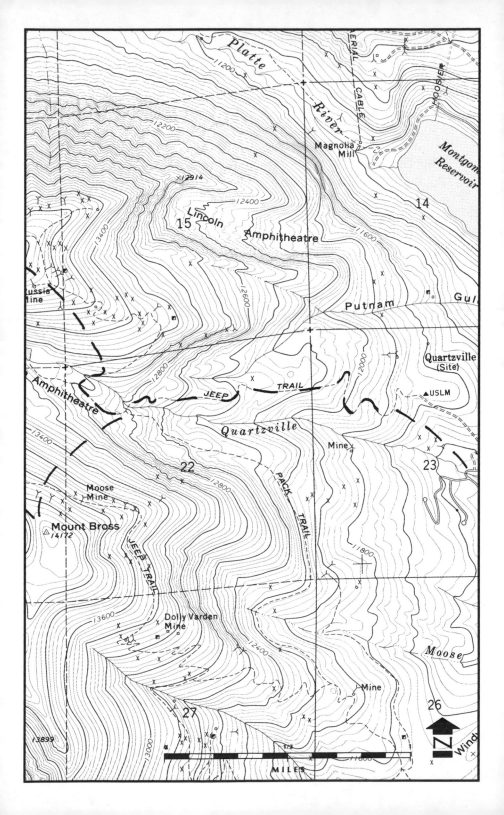

ron-Bross saddle dips to a liveable 13,850 feet. From Bross' summit, descend southwest back to Kite Lake.

Kite Lake to Democrat, Lincoln, and Bross and return: 6 miles, 3,600 feet.

Hoosier Pass Approach

From Alma continue north on Colorado 9 for two miles to where the road begins to climb Hoosier Pass in earnest. A dirt road leads left (west) on Roberts Lane (marked only with faint signs) across the flats for .2 mile and then west for two miles on a road which switchbacks and ends amid a housing development at the mouth of the gulch between Lincoln and Bross a stone's throw from the site of Quartzville. From here climb west northwest up the broad southeast shoulder of Mount Lincoln either via the winding mine road which runs clear to 14,000 feet or straight up the slope. Once on Lincoln, the geography of the route is the same as the Kite Lake approach save for the long pull back from Democrat and then returning northeast off Bross via a good glissade if conditions are right. Is it our imagination or is it always windy and stormy in the Mosquitos? Be prepared.

Road end to Lincoln, Democrat, Bross, and return: 8½ miles, 4,800 feet.

▲

Mount Sherman

14,036 feet (45th highest)

At the southern end of the Mosquito Range, inconspicuously situated near more prominent and easily recognizable Horseshoe Mountain, stands Mount Sherman. Sherman missed the early acclaim of the surveys directed toward Mount Lincoln, and it was apparently 1881 before its name appeared on a map of Colorado. Its namesake appears to have been Civil War veteran General William Tecumseh Sherman. As was the case for all of the Mosquitos, mining activity on the mountain was frenzied, and a first ascent by miners in the 1860s is almost a certainty.

Sherman's greatest claim to fame lies with two once-roaring boom towns and one great mine which lay at its base. Horseshoe, incorporated in 1881, once boasted a post office, two stores, two hotels, a smelter, sawmill, and a population of 300. The real metropolis of the valley, however, was Leavick. Named for Felix Leavick, an early prospector, the town depended on the revenues of the Hilltop mine, located on the southern slopes of Mount Sherman. A two and one-half mile aerial tramway carried buckets of silver ore, 400 pounds per bucket, from the mine shaft to a mill in leavick. The mill still stands in a rapidly deteriorating condition. The silver crash of 1893 brought Hilltop operations to a halt almost overnight, but mine owners soon discovered the mine's potential for yielding high grade zinc ore. Zinc production reached such levels by 1897 that the Denver, South Park and Pacific Railroad built a ten-mile spur from its main line in South Park to Leavick. Much of the grade is visible today.

In 1901, the Hilltop underwent a major renovation which completely electrified the operation and installed new machinery. The *Colorado Mining Directory* of the year showed the Hilltop boasting a 580-foot shaft, 800 feet of drifts, and a work crew of 30 men. Production eventually declined unitl the railroad was abandoned in 1938. Now, only the main mill at Leavick and a few scattered foundations still stand, but as late as the 1940s, Muriel Sibell Wolle, the indomitable sketcher and preserver of ghost-town treasures was able to visit and sketch a valley full of

Mount Sherman from campsite above Leavick. *Gary Koontz.*

reminders of a bustling past.

Mount Sherman's broad summit plateau provided an unexpected landing field for a Cessna 310 which was forced down by severe down-drafts in a violent storm in January of 1967. Pilot Jimmy Williamson of Denver, flying a Clinton Air charter enroute to Aspen, brought the aircraft to rest in deep snow with only minor injuries to his four passengers. Bitter Colorado weather thwarted rescue efforts for 20 hours until a helicopter piloted by Bob Green of Broomfield plucked the group from the peak.

THE ROUTES

Sherman in recent years has become a traditional "first Fourteener" for those wishing to sample the obsession of climbing. Among seasoned Fourteener climbers, the mention of its name brings a chorus of hoots and, occasionally, cheers — take, for example, the intrepid climber on the Little Bear-Blanca ridge who halfway across came up with the bright idea, "Hey, let's do Sherman instead!" But a word of warning — the mountain is still

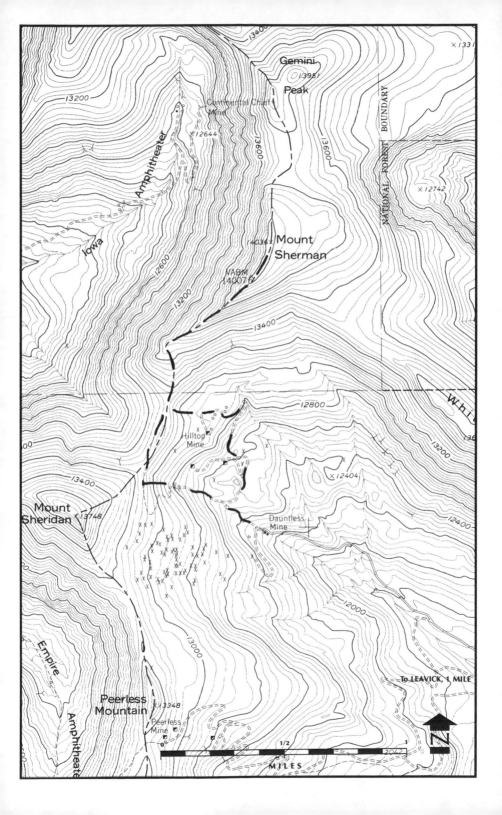

14,000 feet and the unpredictable weather of the Mosquitos makes it a mountain to be respected. (Come to think of it, all mountains should be respected.)

From Fairplay, drive south on U.S. 285 one mile to the Fourmile Creek national forest access road and then right (west) 11 miles on a reasonably good dirt road to Leavick (11,200 feet). At least one winter ski expedition reported the eerie presence of miners' ghosts moving silently about the deserted mine workings to the faint hum of machinery. Leavick is posted with "No Trespassing" signs and camping is best done along the access road within the national forest boundary. From Leavick a jeep road leads west northwest two miles to the Dauntless mine at 12,200 feet. Climb west to the low point of the Sherman-Sheridan saddle and then northeast up the southwest ridge for a total of one and one-half miles and 1,800 feet from the Dauntless. Parties climbing from Leavick may choose a variety of routes up the rolling southern and eastern flanks. In recent years, a key attraction of Sherman's summit has been the large towers of shale rock erected on the summit crest. Yes, folks, there really is enough room up there for a football game!

Leavick to Summit: 3½ miles; 2,800 feet.

▲

Backbone of the Continent:
The Sawatch Range

High, massive, and dominating are three terms which immediately come to mind when describing the Sawatch Range. Anyone who has traveled U.S. 285 and 24 from Salida to Leadville has received a spectacular impression of the Sawatch's nature. Like a row of tremendous granite mammoths, peak upon peak line up to confront the Arkansas Valley — scores of snow-clad summits tower up to 6,000 feet above the river. Fifteen Fourteeners rise in the Sawatch, including the three highest peaks of the Rockies, more than any other range in the contiguous forty-eight states. In a very real sense, the Sawatch is the backbone of the continent.

The Sawatch Range averages about 20 miles in width and stretches from the Eagle River south for 90 miles to Antora Mountain. Bounding the Sawatch are some of Colorado's great rivers; the Arkansas on the east, the Eagle on the north, the Roaring Fork on the northwest, and the Taylor and Gunnison drainages on the west. The Continental Divide is an integral part of the Sawatch's geography, entering the northern part near Tennessee Pass and running the remaining length of the range to south of Marshall Pass.

The Sawatch Range is indeed a physically impressive range, but unlike the Tetons, for example, Sawatch peaks are generally more impressive for their massiveness and over-all altitude than their ruggedness. Nevertheless, there are a number of localities in the Sawatch, such as the areas around Ice Mountain, La Plata Peak, and the Mount of the Holy Cross, that equal any of the ranges in Colorado for alpine ruggedness in the form of great rock faces and bristling ridges.

Geologically, the Sawatch Range is quite straightforward, being essentially a faulted anticline with Tertiary intrusions and one extrusion. The largest and most important intrusion was the

Princeton Batholith, which extends the width of the range from Mount Princeton to Mount Shavano. This batholith is composed largely of granite and quartz monzonite and is responsible for both the "Chalk" Cliffs of Mount Princeton and the gem field of Mount Antero.

Associated with this Tertiary igneous activity was the mineralization of much of the Sawatch Range. Silver, lead, gold, and other minerals crystallized into many of the cracks and fissures in the Precambrian core of the Sawatch, forming veins which became the attraction for hordes of fortune-seekers, beginning in the 1860s. Silver was the most commonly mined mineral in the Sawatch, but the best deposits of both silver and gold lay just beyond the outer slopes of the Sawatch peaks in such locations as Leadville, Aspen, and Tincup.

By 1880, numerous mining camps had grown up in almost every valley of the Sawatch. In addition, crude roads were constructed up the valleys and even across the range to connect with mining camps west of the divide. Monarch, Tincup, Cottonwood, Independence, and Marshall passes were just a few of the routes used by miners to reach the vast country of the Western Slope.

Many of the Sawatch peaks were undoubtedly first climbed and named by miners in the 1870s. The name "Sawatch" appears as early as 1853, apparently a derivation from an Indian word meaning "water of the blue earth," and originally applied to a large lake which once existed in the San Luis Valley.

Concurrent with the mining activity was a comprehensive survey of the Sawatch, undertaken in 1873, as part of Ferdinand Vandeveer Hayden's larger survey of the West, under the auspices of the United States Department of the Interior. Hayden's men climbed a number of Sawatch giants, including Elbert, Massive, La Plata, and Harvard.

The dire need for cheap transportation into the booming mining camps of western Colorado drew narrow-gauge railroads into the Sawatch by 1880. General William Jackson Palmer's Denver and Rio Grande Railway and John Evans' Denver, South Park, and Pacific became involved in a great race to be the first to throw rails across the Sawatch and tap the wealth of the Gunnison country. The only standard-gauge railroad to cross the Sawatch was the Colorado Midland, boring under the Continental

Divide with Hagerman Tunnel, west of Leadville, in 1887.

Recent history in the Sawatch has focused on water diversion projects. Small diversion ditches in the vicinity of Tennessee Pass captured and transported water from the Western Slope to the Arkansas Valley in the early 1900s. The largest diversion project in the range is the Twin Lakes facility, completed in 1935 as part of the New Deal. Most recently, the Homestake Project was built to divert upper Eagle River water for use by the communities of Aurora and Colorado Springs.

Mount of the Holy Cross
14,005 feet (52nd highest)

The aura of legend, history, and religious significance which
has surrounded the Mount of the Holy Cross makes it one of the
most notable of all of the peaks in Colorado, and perhaps even
the United States. Isolated in the heart of the northern Sawatch
and hidden from the east by Notch Mountain, the peak was
enveloped in an air of mystery for years, and many felt that the
huge white cross upon its side was more legend than fact. Upon
verification of its existence, however, the peak vaulted into the
national limelight, overnight becoming a grand symbol of the
Christian faith. Thousands of photographic reproductions and
paintings of the peak were circulated world-wide, and for a few
years, Christians in the United States had a site to which they
could make a bona fide pilgrimage within their own country.

The cross itself lies on the northeast face of the peak and is
composed of a vertical couloir 25 to 50 feet wide and 1,500 feet
long. The horizontal arm of the cross is approximately 750 feet
long and is an outward-sloping bench which collects more snow
than the steeper surrounding rock face. Geologically, the upright
of the cross was formed from the weathering of a seam of schist,
which was much less resistant than the gneiss which bordered
on either side. While the cross has lost some of its grandeur
today, it is still obviously a cross formation and still impressive.

The origins of the naming of the Mount of the Holy Cross
are extremely obscure, rooted more deeply in legend than in
supportable fact. A number of legends deal with sighting of the
cross by early Spanish explorers. Another legend claims discovery
by lost priests from New Mexico in the 1700s. Like most legends,
however, these stories are not supportable by facts. Holy Cross
was probably first sighted from a distance by an unknown trapper
or miner who reported his sighting to someone else who embel-
lished the story, and gradually the mysterious mountain became
known by word of mouth.

The first official sighting of the peak was by William H.
Brewer, who ascended Grays Peak on August 29, 1869. He de-

Looking south on the approach to the Mount of the Holy Cross. The cross couloir is out of sight behind the left-hand ridge, and the traditional route follows the right-hand ridge.

scribed the view from the summit, and his casual reference to the Mount of the Holy Cross, far in the distance, indicates that by 1869, the mountain was fairly well known, although its location was not yet pinpointed.

In 1873, the Hayden Survey made locating the Mount of the Holy Cross one of its primary objectives. The fascinating account of the discovery and the most complete work on the Mount of the Holy Cross is Robert L. Brown's *Holy Cross — The Mountain and the City*. Briefly, William Henry Jackson, the famed western photographer, was the main character in the story. Jackson traveled with the Hayden Survey in 1873 as the official photographer, and on August 23, after numerous false starts and great difficulty passing through fallen timber, Jackson ascended Notch Mountain and took the now-famous first photographs of the cross. Meanwhile, J. T. Gardner and W. H. Holmes achieved the first ascent of the mountain itself. When the team returned to civilization with the news of their discovery and the photographs, the fame of the peak was inevitable.

A measure of the peak's sudden rise to fame can be seen by noting its incorporation into the arts soon after its discovery. Thomas Moran, the noted English artist and painter of Western scenes, was greatly inspired by Jackson's original photographs and made a trip to the peak himself in 1874. Afterward, Moran completed a number of paintings featuring the legendary mountain, the best of which measures 7 feet, 10 inches by 6 feet and now hangs in England. Other smaller originals also exist, and countless reproductions are found throughout the world.

In 1880, free gold was discovered not far to the east of the Mount of the Holy Cross, and placer discoveries were made along Homestake Creek, south of the mountain. With these discoveries, the Holy Cross Mining District was established, and several hastily built communities appeared. One community was located in the Homestake drainage just four miles south of the Mount of the Holy Cross. While the peak itself was not visible from the camp, it soon acquired the name of Holy Cross City, anyway. Mines such as the Pelican, Molly, Comstock, and Treasure Vault produced enough ore to attract about 300 people to the community. The town itself consisted of two rows of houses, two general stores, the Timberline Hotel, two saloons, and a hodgepodge of other buildings.

Despite a promising beginning, Holy Cross City was doomed to fade after only four years because of the severe winters, poor transportation in such a remote area, and a slowdown in mineral production. Brief resurgences of activity occurred in the late 1890s and in 1927, but these were minor, and Holy Cross City has been a true ghost town since about 1900.

In 1912, O. W. Daggett and Cole McDougal climbed the peak via the most direct route — the upright of the cross. Their hopes of a possible first ascent by this route were dashed, however, when they discovered a 200-foot-long climbing rope which had been left in the upper part of the cross. Other ascents up the cross were made by experienced parties in the years that followed, and numerous new rock routes were pioneered on the east face.

Also in 1912, the forerunner of the famous Holy Cross pilgrimages took place when three Episcopal priests held Eucharist on the summit of Notch Mountain. The organized pilgrimages began in the 1920s, largely due to the efforts of Father John P. Carrigan of Glenwood Springs. In 1928, 218 persons went on the pilgrimage to Notch Mountain; by 1932, the number had grown to 2,000. By this time, the entire area around the mountain had taken on a sacred air. A snow formation to the right of the cross became known as the Supplicating Virgin, and a lake at the base of the mountain was the Bowl of Tears. In addition, many miraculous healings were reported by either actual pilgrims or by those who had sent their handkerchiefs with those of the pilgrimage, a practice taken from scripture. Ironically, in 1938, just as these pilgrimages were at their height, they were halted by the United States Army, which controlled the surrounding area as a military reservation until 1950.

In 1929, the Mount of the Holy Cross National Monument was established by President Herbert Hoover, but was abolished in 1950. The reason for this status loss was the reported deterioration of the right arm of the cross. Some claim that the arm has not deteriorated at all, but that the quality of the cross merely fluctuates from year to year depending on sun, wind, and snow deposition. However, it is likely that some degree of deterioration has occurred from rockslides. Nevertheless, in 1951, a stamp honoring Colorado's 75th anniversary was issued which featured the peak with its cross in perfect form. Interestingly, in more than a hundred years since its discovery, the cross has apparently never been in as fine a form as when William Henry Jackson took those first photographs in 1873.

In recent years, climbing Holy Cross has been increasingly popular, but a winter ascent was not accomplished until 1966. On January 1 of that year, inspired in part by a $1966 prize offered by Holy Cross College of Worcester, Massachusetts, four seniors from that institution reached the summit along with a Vail guide. This ascent made Holy Cross one of the last Colorado Fourteeners to be climbed in winter, a feat accomplished by relatively few since that time.

On July 8, 1973, a tragic fatality and a daring rescue took place on the upright of the cross. Dick Boss and Ron Dillon were roped together, descending the cross, when Boss slipped and began sliding down the treacherous couloir. Having lost control of his ice axe, he could not self-arrest, and Dillon prepared to arrest his partner's fall. The momentum of Boss's body was too great, however, and soon both were racing wildly down the

snow. Near the bottom of the cross, a cliff appeared, and both went hurtling over the edge. Boss was killed on the impact, but miraculously, Dillon was thrown clear from the cliff and landed injured but alive in the snow 200 feet below. Other climbers in the party went for help, and hours later, a dramatic effort by helicopter pilot Len Casdorf rescued Dillon, who later spent a month recuperating in a Denver hospital. This incident reinforces the fact that the Mount of the Holy Cross, while a beautiful peak and one with a fascinating history, can be dangerous to those who venture onto its northeast face and are not well experienced in mountaineering techniques.

T H E   R O U T E S

Half Moon Campground
From two miles south of Minturn on U.S. 24, just before the highway crosses the Eagle River and begins to climb Battle Mountain, turn west for six miles to Tigiwon Campground and two more miles to Half Moon Campground (10,400 feet). The road is passable in cars and climbs on switchbacks through aspen and pine. From Half Moon Campground, the trail leads two miles to Half Moon Pass (11,600 feet) and then descends two miles and 900 feet to East Cross Creek. The descent is a welcome relief on the approach — but oh, those 900 feet are murder on the way out for the ill-conditioned! Near the trail crossing of East Cross Creek, there are a number of serene campsites; however, the area's high use demands extra discretion and care when choosing a site. From here, the easiest route follows the trail across East Cross Creek, skirts west of the cliffs on Holy Cross's north ridge, and then climbs along the broad north ridge to the summit. The ridge may also be reached by going up the rocky gulch at the base of the north ridge cliffs and then angling southwest to the ridge crest once in the basin beneath the main peak. This route is steeper and involves some bushwhacking low in the gulch.

A direct approach via the cross involves a 1,500-foot technical snow and ice climb and should be attempted only by experienced parties fully cognizant of rock and avalanche conditions.

NOTE: As of 1988, the U.S. Forest Service is considering

limiting day access to Holy Cross as well as initiating a permit system for camping. Forest Service inquiries are advised.

Half Moon Campground to Summit: 7 miles, 4,500 feet (plus 900 feet on the return).

▲

Mount Massive
14,421 feet (2nd highest)

Massive — there's really no other name for it. With five main points above 14,000 feet and a broad three-mile summit crest, the mountain *is* massive. Henry Gannett climbed, named, and mapped the mountain for the Hayden Survey in 1873. Little did he know that the name he gave it, despite its appropriateness, would cause so much fervor in the years ahead.

By 1880, Leadville, at the mountain's base, was a booming silver camp eagerly awaiting the arrival of not just one, but two railroads. As the fortunes of Horace Tabor, Molly Brown, and Baby Doe rose and fell, Leadville residents became quite fond of "old Massive." Its presence was felt on the town year-round — from the warm sunbeams of a cool summer morning first kissing its summit, to the bone-chilling, below-zero nights when bitter winds from its slopes sent snow piling up a dozen feet. Yup, it was massive all right!

With such an appropriate name, it was only a matter of time before someone would suggest changing it! The first attempt occurred in 1901, when the *Denver Post* thought it would be "most appropriate" to rename the peak "Mount McKinley" after the then recently assassinated President William McKinley. The *Leadville Herald-Democrat* immediately championed a petition drive against the change. The petition, which soon boasted a thousand local signatures, was sent to the U.S. Board of Geographic Names. The Board's chairman replied that he agreed with local sentiment — after all, there already was one Mount McKinley and the name, "Massive," was very descriptive. The chairman's name was Henry Gannett.

Doubtless Gannett would have voiced a similar opinion some twenty years later when another attempt was made to rename the peak none other than "Gannett Peak." A six-year fight by the Colorado Mountain Club and Leadville residents finally reversed a preliminary decision to call the peak "Gannett," and the name "Massive" was restored.

Mount Massive from the east, showing that the mountain is indeed massive. *Colorado Historical Society.*

In 1965, State Senator John Bermingham, R-Denver, tried to turn a "Third-Time's-the-Charm" by seeking to rename the peak "Mount Churchill" in honor of the late Sir Winston Churchill. While Massive's character was well suited to that of England's most famous "bulldog," local sentiment again prevailed, and the proposal was defeated. Hopefully, once and for all, Massive's name is secure.

T H E   R O U T E S

North Halfmoon Creek
From Malta, three miles west of Leadville on U.S. 24, at the collection of trailers, take Colorado 300 west one mile, then south and southwest along Halfmoon Creek five miles to Halfmoon Campground (10,000 feet). (Follow signs.) Three and one-half miles beyond the campground, the road (passable in cars) forks just before crossing Halfmoon Creek. Park cars (10,500 feet) and hike northwest along a well-developed trail along North

Halfmoon Creek for one and one-half miles. Here, North Half-moon Creek swings almost due west, and a prominent gulch leads almost due north to the saddle between the summit and southern sub-peak (14,132 feet). The true summit is one-half mile north of the saddle.

Avoid climbing to the ridge (to the right and east when heading up the valley) even by the inviting gully which forks northeast at the junction described above. This will take you into a steep section just southwest of the sub-peak and will require a climb over its summit.

Trailhead to Summit: 3 miles; 3,900 feet.

A more scenic route bears left (west) with North Halfmoon Creek from the junction described above for one-half mile and then abruptly north again along the creek to the lower of two high lakes. From here, follow the drainage to the east which leads directly to Massive's main summit. It may be desirable to angle slightly to the right (southeast) and hit the summit ridge just south of the summit. This avoids the steep upper section of the west face, but takes you into the shadow of a north-facing slope and may require ice axes early in the year.

Trailhead to Summit: 4 miles; 3,900 feet.

Mount Massive Trail

At the Main Range Trail's junction with the Halfmoon Creek road, one and one-half miles west of the campground, hike north on the Main Range Trail for three miles to a west (left) junction with the Mount Massive Trail at 11,250 feet. Follow the trail west for another four miles to the summit. This trail route, while long, is probably the preferable one for large parties and those with children.

Trailhead to Summit: 7 miles; 4,400 feet.

For the adventuresome backpacker, try a western approach to Massive from the Fryingpan Lakes in the remote upper reaches of the Fryingpan River. The ascent east of the lakes is steep and involves climbing 14,320-foot North Massive first, but could prove to be a real "wilderness classic."

▲

Mount Elbert

14,433 feet (Highest point in Colorado)

Of the 3,000 miles of Rocky Mountain peaks, only one can claim the honor of being the highest, Colorado's Mount Elbert. In addition, only California's 14,495-foot Mount Whitney is higher in the contiguous 48 states. Mount Elbert rises above the Arkansas Valley in a gigantic mass whose most distinguishing characteristics are its long, smooth ridges. Consequently, Mount Elbert gives the appearance of a mountain at rest, seemingly comfortably confident of its status as the monarch of the Rockies.

Although some question surrounds the exact date of its naming, it was the namesake of Samuel Elbert, who first came to Colorado Territory in 1862 as secretary to Governor John Evans. Elbert furthered his political fortune in 1865 by marrying Evans' daughter, Josephine. In March of 1873, after serving in the territorial legislature, he was appointed territorial governor by President Ulysses S. Grant. Elbert served an inglorious term of less than one year between two controversial terms of Edward McCook — terms marked by the best of the Grant Administration scandal. Such service by Elbert hardly deserved recognition on Colorado's tallest mountain, but Elbert did go on to serve 20 years on the State Supreme Court after statehood was granted in 1876.

Not only has Mount Elbert's role as the Colorado high point made it suffer the indignity of countless tests of its altitude, but also the peak has witnessed just about every assault imaginable. Elbert's first documented ascent was by H.W. Stuckle of the Hayden Survey in 1874. In recent years, however, its summit has been reached by jeep, bicycle, all-terrain vehicles, and even helicopter, when a *Denver Post* photographer delivered an evening edition under a rock at the summit cairn, presumably to a literate pika. Despite years of talk, Elbert never has had a road built to its summit. Hopefully, this is one indignity it will never have to suffer!

Mount Elbert's traditional pose with its prominent eastern cirque and northeast ridge.

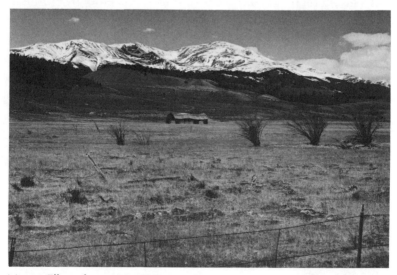

Mount Elbert from U.S. 285 near Granite.

T H E   R O U T E S

Mount Elbert can be and has been climbed from virtually every point on the compass.

Halfmoon Creek

From Halfmoon Campground (see Mount Massive), drive or hike west one and one-half miles to the junction with the Main Range Trail (10,060 feet), where camping is also available. The sign at the trailhead speaks of the Mount Elbert Trail junction being five miles, and from the junction, it is about another three miles up the east ridge of the summit. However, if you desire to climb Mount Elbert by the Mount Elbert Trail, a shorter and better approach is probably made from Twin Lakes. From Halfmoon Creek, however, there is a much shorter and equally easy route up Elbert via an unnamed trail up its northeast ridge.

For the northeast ridge trail, proceed up the Main Range Trail to the south, crossing Elbert Creek and then climbing southeast to the top of a ridge (10,600 feet). The Main Range Trail then levels out for about one-half mile, and you can relax in preparation for the remaining 3,800 vertical feet. When the Main Range Trail appears to drop more steeply into the Box Creek Valley, don't panic; just continue following it on down for another quarter-mile where an obvious but unsigned fork is met. Take the right-hand fork here which angles upslope rather than continuing on the Main Range Trail which continues dropping slightly to cross Box Creek before long, eventually joining the Mount Elbert Trail.

Follow the right-hand trail west as it climbs steeply to timberline, one mile distant. From timberline, the trail continues and gains Elbert's northeast ridge at about 12,700 feet. From here, it is simply a climb up the northeast ridge to the right (northwest) of the Box Creek cirque and on to the gentle summit, one and one-half miles.

Trailhead to Summit: 4½ miles; 4,400 feet.

Halfmoon Creek also offers an approach from the northwest. Continue two miles west from the Main Range Trail-road junction to where South Halfmoon Creek enters the main stream from the south (10,285 feet). Hike south up South Halfmoon Creek into the valley between French Peak (13,922 feet), a prominent thir-

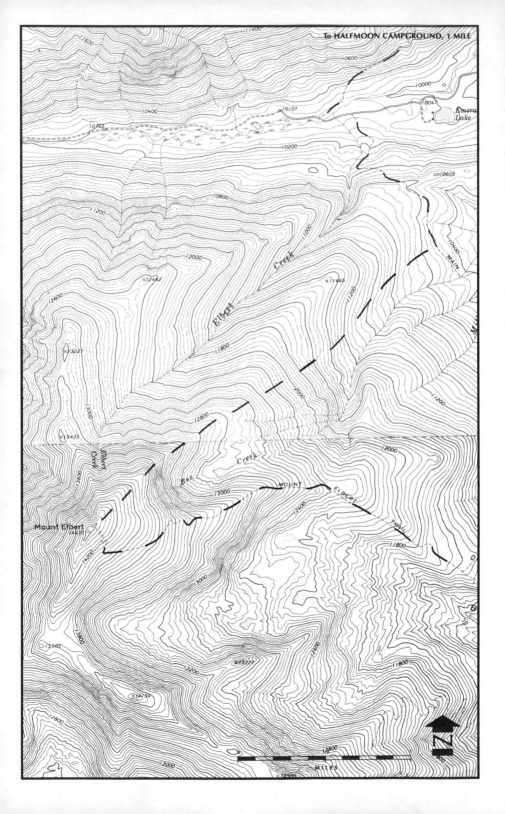

To HALFMOON CAMPGROUND, 1 MILE

teener, and Elbert. After a good two miles up the valley, Elbert may be climbed by any of a number of prominent west face gullies.

Main Range Trail Junction to Summit: 5½ miles; 4,400 feet.

Echo Canyon, Bull Hill

While longer than the Halfmoon Creek routes, this approach has a number of scenic and historical attractions, plus the added incentive of frequently fewer people. From the town of Twin Lakes on Colorado 82, drive west up the winding road toward Independence Pass for six miles to the mouth of Echo Canyon, about a mile west past Monitor Rock (marked with sign). Here, a north-side pullout and several large cabins mark the bottom of an old tramway cut which once hauled ore from mines high on Bull Hill to the road along Lake Creek. From the bottom of the tramway cut, hike north to the top of the tram and follow old mining roads to a cluster of buildings, remnants of the old Champion and Last Chance mines. Continue north and northeast on the ridge, skirting Bull Hill to the east to save as much elevation gain and drop as possible, then up Elbert's broad south ridge to the highest point in the state, for a total of five miles. On the return, skirting Bull Hill still means an elevation gain of several hundred feet. (Recent changes in private property may restrict access near the mouth of Echo Canyon.)

Tramway base to Summit: 5 miles, 5,000 feet; 500 feet on return to top of Bull Hill.

▲

La Plata Peak

14,336 feet (5th highest)

La Plata Peak rises six miles south of Mount Elbert among the row of mountains which separates Lake and Clear creeks. Unlike many of its neighbors, La Plata has a rugged personality all of its own, and thus stands out in the midst of many less dramatic Sawatch peaks. Being such an impressive mountain, La Plata has long captured the attention of both the casual traveler and the serious mountaineer.

It is probable that La Plata was first ascended by miners in the late 1860s or early 1870s, for numerous high silver mines were located in its vicinity, especially to the south. However, the first recorded climb was made by members of the Hayden Survey on July 26, 1873, who gave the peak its name, which means "silver" in Spanish. William N. Byers, the colorful editor of the *Rocky Mountain News*, and no stranger to mountaineering, accompanied this portion of the survey and sent running accounts to be published in his Denver paper. Byers followed Chief Topographer James Gardner and others to the summit via the northwest ridge and noted with vivid description the abundance of raspberries, strawberries, and sky-blue forget-me-nots found far above timberline. Upon reaching the summit, Byers was awed with the magnificent view and wrote, "The world seems made of mountains; a chaotic mass of rocky ridges, peaks and spurs," a description every Colorado mountaineer readily understands.

The most spectacular single feature of La Plata Peak is its northeast ridge, an incredibly narrow, rugged, and exposed two-mile collection of pinnacles, cuts, and rock faces. This ridge was quite naturally avoided by the early climbers of La Plata, but as climbing techniques became more sophisticated in the 1900s, it was destined that the challenge of this ragged ridge would soon lure some daring climber into attempting it. That daring climber was Albert R. Ellingwood.

Albert Ellingwood probably contributed more to the development of technical climbing in Colorado than any other person. Born in 1888 in Iowa, Ellingwood attended high school in Col-

Looking south to La Plata Peak from the summit of Mount Elbert; Ellingwood Ridge is in the foreground. *Lyndon J. Lampert.*

Gary Kocsis surveys La Plata Peak during first winter ascent of peak's
Ellingwood Ridge. *Craig F. Koontz.*

orado Springs; in 1910, he was awarded a Rhodes Scholarship. After being graduated from Oxford with a degree in civil law, Ellingwood taught as a professor of political science in Colorado and Illinois, and from 1931 until his death in 1934, he was an Assistant Dean at Northwestern University.

While in England attending Oxford, Ellingwood engaged in rock climbing and soon learned the virtues of safe climbing techniques with the use of a rope. He brought this invaluable knowledge back to the States, and in the years that followed, he was able to pioneer many climbs previously thought to be "impossible." Included in these were the first ascents of the Crestones, Lizard Head, Middle Teton, South Teton, and what was only the third ascent of the Grand Teton. In addition, Ellingwood pioneered many new routes on other peaks, such as the Ellingwood Arete on the Crestone Needle and the threatening northeast ridge of La Plata Peak, now appropriately named "Ellingwood Ridge."

Ellingwood met the challenge of the ridge which would one day bear his name in 1921. Climbing with Robert Ormes and two others, Ellingwood departed from the rest of the party to attack the ridge solo, and was not heard from until he showed up at camp late in the evening. Ellingwood had conquered the ridge and gleefully reported that he had dangled from a finger ledge for two full minutes. He obviously enjoyed the tricky problems of technical mountaineering, and it was not long before Ellingwood Ridge became renowned as one of the classic technical climbs of the Sawatch.

In the years that followed, numerous parties succeeded in making summer ascents of Ellingwood Ridge, but all attempts at a grueling winter ascent failed. On March 19, 1960, Karl Pfiffner, George Hurley, and Ron Bierstadt began climbing Ellingwood Ridge, but they were forced to retreat due to oncoming darkness. On the descent, at about timberline, the trio entered a small, steep basin. An extremely cold winter followed by a sudden warming trend had produced a deep layer of unstable hoar snow beneath the surface crust, and the snow of the basin slid, carrying with it all three men. Hurley and Bierstadt quickly extricated themselves, but their partner Pfiffner could not be found. His body was finally located by a rescue party at the foot of the 300-foot-long slide the following morning, bringing to a conclu-

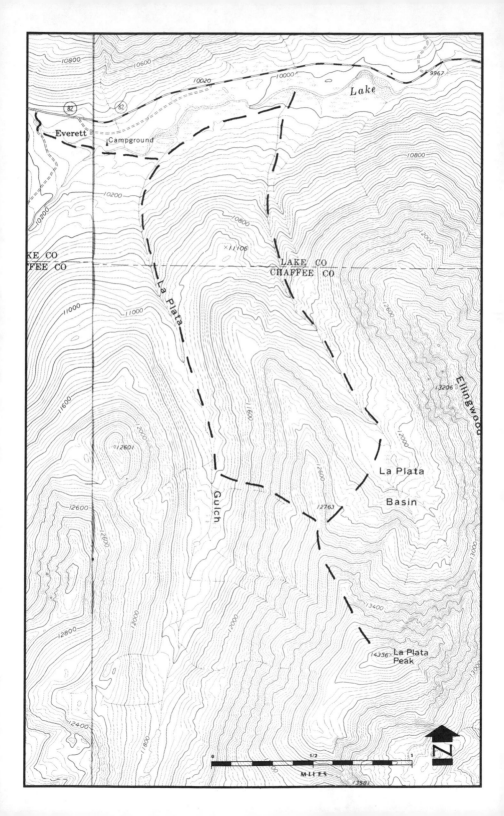

sion this tragedy of the only reported fatal avalanche involved in a climb of a Colorado Fourteener.

The Pfiffner accident put a damper on winter attempts of Ellingwood Ridge until January 12, 1974, when Craig Koontz, Gary Kocsis, Chuck Tolton, and John Lafferty began an assault on the ridge. The experienced team had planned a two-day climb, but hampered by strong winds, snow-covered pitches, and difficult route-finding, it extended far longer. Finally, on the afternoon of January 15, after four days on the ridge, the four men stood on the summit of La Plata Peak, and one of Colorado's last great winter ascents was a reality.

Approximately seven miles to the west of La Plata Peak is Grizzly Peak, lying on the Continental Divide. Grizzly was formerly rated at an even 14,000 feet, but in 1965, the U.S. Geological Survey revised this figure to 13,988 feet. Nevertheless, even though it is now out of the Fourteener club, Grizzly deserves mention as a notable mountain well worth climbing.

Grizzly Peak, like La Plata, was probably first climbed by miners in search of silver, but the first recorded ascent was made by members of the Hayden Survey. Reportedly, they observed a grizzly bear floating on an iceberg in a lake at the base of this peak, resulting in the name. Unfortunately, the several Colorado mountains which bear the name of "Grizzly" are somewhat of anachronisms, as the silvertips are in all probability extinct in the state.

T H E   R O U T E S

La Plata Gulch

From the junction of U.S. 24 and Colorado 82, drive west on Colorado 82 for 14 miles to the junction of Lake Creek and its South Fork. Here, a dirt road leads south across a wooden bridge over Lake Creek. Park in the wide area just west of the intersection and walk south on the dirt road. Immediately across the bridge, an unmarked path leads east (left) along the south side of Lake Creek. Follow the path or its minor variations for a quarter-mile to near the major obstacle of the climb — the South Fork of Lake Creek. The described path network ends on the old campground road as it curves south perhaps several hundred yards south of Lake Creek. Do not follow the road south, but rather at its easternmost point, hike east several hundred yards toward the sound of the South Fork. (Do not follow main Lake Creek to the South Fork confluence.) The South Fork has cut several different channels over the years, but currently the main eastern channel is crossed by a crude and exposed log bridge just before the stream plunges into a small gorge above its confluence with Lake Creek. Given the exposure, a fixed rope across the log may be desirable. Once across the South Fork, continue east along the south side of Lake Creek for almost one-half mile to La Plata Gulch Creek. A trail runs south along the east side of the gulch for two miles to timberline. Then, angle east (left) to La Plata's northwest ridge, 1,600 steep feet above. Once on the ridge, the summit is less than one mile south.

South Fork Bridge to Summit: 4 miles; 4,200 feet.

La Plata Basin

An alternate route, not as steep, but culminating on the same northwest ridge, is via La Plata Basin, one mile east of La Plata Gulch. This basin may be reached by traveling one mile east from the South Fork along the south side of Lake Creek as described above. Pick your way south through the timber and up the slope for one and one-half miles into the basin. At the southwest corner of the basin, a broad couloir which passes north of prominent cliffs is the simplest route to the low point in the northwest ridge, which then leads south one mile to the summit. This route may be done directly south from Colorado 82 if passage over the oft-swollen Lake Creek can be found, either by log jam or snow bridge in the winter. Private property changes may restrict access for the direct approach.

South Fork Bridge to Summit: 4½ miles; 4,200 feet.

Direct from 82: 3 miles; 4,300 feet.

One additional possibility for La Plata is, of course, Ellingwood Ridge, but it is recommended only for experienced, technical climbers. Several rappels may be involved as well as a 40-foot jam crack. Most prefer to admire the nasty ridge from a distance and leave its ascent to the Albert Ellingwoods.

▲

Mount Oxford
14,153 feet (27th highest)

Mount Belford
14,197 feet (19th highest)

Missouri Mountain
14,067 feet (36th highest)

While the attention of the surveys focused on Mount Elbert and Mount Harvard, a ridge of three fourteen-thousand-foot-plus points, rising between the two, was largely ignored. The three peaks, resembling the gentle, rolling humps of a camel, were mapped in the Hayden Atlas but not named. Indeed, a key reason for the scant attention they received is their lack of any distinctive or striking features.

During the silver boom of the early 1880s, miners rode up Clear Creek north of the peaks and established a string of boom towns, Beaver City, Silverdale, Vicksburg, Rockdale, and Winfield. Today, only the remnants of Vicksburg and Winfield survive, testaments to the preservation work of the Clear Creek Canyon Historical Society of Chaffee County. Society members have restored a number of buildings in an attempt to keep packrat, souvenir hunters from carrying the towns off piece by piece to a thousand backyards scattered across the country.

Sometime during the mining rush, miners from the "Show Me" state of Missouri decided to show locals their fondness for the folks back home, and Missouri Gulch, Missouri Basin, and Missouri Mountain, the westernmost of the three peaks, were named. Which came first is a case of the proverbial chicken and the egg; history has recorded no better explanation.

Likewise, history cannot pinpoint a date when some barrel-chested miner swung his pick into the ground and declared, "By

Mount Belford looking south up Missouri Gulch.

gum, let's name that thar peak for old Jim Belford." James B. Belford was Colorado's first U.S. Congressman after statehood was achieved and a powerful voice for the free coinage of silver. Belford's flaming red hair and fiery oratory earned him the nickname of "The Red-Headed Rooster of the Rockies." The miners followed Belford's silver speeches with keen interest and in time his name became associated with the peak identifiable by its reddish rock outcropping on the summit. Prospect holes cover the mountain, including the very summit, and are evidence that the miners were very familiar with the land above timberline.

Recognition of the Oxford, Belford, and Missouri massif received a boost in 1925 when Albert Ellingwood (see La Plata Peak) and Stephen H. Hart took transit sightings on "an unnamed mountain with three summits of 14,000 feet altitude north and east [*sic*] of Mount Harvard" from the summits of Harvard and Columbia. Six years later, in 1931, John L. Jerome Hart, brother of Stephen, pondered over naming the peak while compiling his classic *Fourteen Thousand Feet*. In keeping with Collegiate Peaks tradition, he christened it "Mount Oxford" after the university

Mount Oxford looking southeast from Belford's north ridge. Mount Harvard is visible over the Oxford-Belford saddle at the extreme right. *Gary Koontz.*

Missouri Mountain from the slopes of Mount Belford looking west. The summit is the hump above the prominent "C-shaped" snowfield.

attended by Ellingwood and Stephen Hart. By no small coincidence, John Hart was also a Rhodes Scholar. Both Hart brothers became eminent Denver lawyers and public servants, Stephen Hart as Chairman of the Board of the Colorado Historical Society and John Hart as President of the American Alpine Club.

While their broad ridges and gentle slopes make Oxford and Belford rather dull mountains for the more adventurous climber, both peaks are exceptionally good beginner or family climbs. Missouri Mountain, however, offers an exception to the broad, gentle ridge description, and on one occasion, it tragically snuffed out the lives of two climbers. On Saturday, July 3, 1976, Kim Wickholm, 21, and Sharon Barnes, 29, fell to their deaths down a northeast-face couloir. Some mystery surrounds the accident; one possible explanation is that the couple reached the summit in the fading twilight via an easy route and then in an attempt to get off the mountain by darkness tried to descend the steep couloir. The fact that Wickholm was an experienced climber and that both were well equipped only deepens the mystery.

T H E   R O U T E S

Missouri Gulch, Oxford and Belford

From U.S. 24, 14 miles north of Buena Vista, turn left (west) at Clear Creek Reservoir and drive eight miles to Vicksburg (9,700 feet). Camping spots are available that do not disrupt the restoration of the town undertaken by the Clear Creek Historical Society. From Vicksburg, cross Clear Creek south on a Forest Service bridge and hike two miles south into upper Missouri Gulch Basin. The first half-mile is steep, but abundant Colorado columbines make for enticing rest stops. From the basin angle southeast up Belford's northwest ridge to the right (southwest) of the prominent couloir. Once on Belford, Oxford is a one-and-one-half-mile walk northeast through a saddle that costs 700 feet of elevation. From both Oxford and Belford, a particularly impressive view of Harvard appears. Rising above broad Missouri Basin, Harvard's size and dimensions are far more accented than when viewed from the south.

Vicksburg to Belford: 3 miles; 4,500 feet.

Vicksburg to Belford plus Oxford: 4½ miles; 5,200 feet.

From Oxford, a tempting glissade may be had northwest

into Belford Gulch for the descent; *however,* the pleasure of upper Belford Gulch gives way to the cold task of crossing Clear Creek minus a bridge. In high water, a rope is a necessity. Groups with small children or beginners should make the 700-foot vertical backtrack over Belford to Missouri Gulch.

Missouri Mountain

From the high basin at the head of Missouri Gulch, Missouri Mountain is the long ridge to the southwest. The highest point is barely discernible as the third point to the right (west) of the low pass at the head (south) of the basin (Elkhead Pass). Angle southwest to the ridge up any number of couloirs to the right (northwest) of the summit. The couloirs directly below and to the left (east) of the summit can be climbed but require ice axes. If spring conditions are right, melting snow will form a huge "C" at the top of the couloir just below the summit — a good route for those properly equipped.

Vicksburg to Missouri: 4 miles; 4,400 feet.

Missouri seems a good peak from which to preach the gospel of the ice axe. Although definitely not needed on a number of summer climbs, ice axes are invaluable to the serious climber. Although their presence is frequently sneered at by people not understanding their importance, they are part of the authors' climbing gear 365 days a year. In 1972, Omar Richardson and Walt Borneman were caught in a mid-July thunderstorm (one which struck at 11:00 A.M.) atop Missouri. After failing to find a route off the peak east toward Elkhead Pass (there are several pitches requiring rope), the pair reclimbed several hundred feet in freezing rain to the summit. With lightning flashing around them, they made a hurried exit down a long shoestring couloir just east of the summit. The snow was hardpacked with an icy crust, but a thousand-foot glissade with ice axe heads buried through the crust dropped the climbers out of danger within several minutes. Descending the couloir without an ice axe would have resulted in a thousand-foot death ride.

Ice axes make for safer, surer climbing and also have numerous supplemental uses. So, carry an ice axe and know how to use it!

Meanwhile, back on Missouri Mountain, the peak can also

be climbed via an interesting backpack route which continues south up Missouri Gulch and crosses Elkhead Pass into upper Missouri *Basin*. From there, Missouri is climbed by going west to the saddle between (south of) Missouri and Iowa Peak (13,831 feet) and then northeast to the summit. Missouri Basin also offers southern routes to Oxford and Belford and is entered from U.S. 24 about 12 miles north of Buena Vista up Pine Creek.

▲

Huron Peak

14,005 feet (53rd highest)

Bounded on three sides by beautiful valleys, Huron Peak was probably first climbed by prospectors from one of the mining camps in the Clear Creek Valley. Many substantial mines were located in the area, and numerous prospect holes dot the mountain. Although not a particularly historic peak, Huron does offer one of the best views in the Sawatch Range.

The exact origin of Huron's name is unknown, but John L.J. Hart reported that it was probably named for a Huron mine somewhere in the vicinity. A relative latecomer to the Fourteener rolls, Huron was not given official U.S. Geological Survey designation until 1956.

From the summit of Huron, the valleys of Clear Creek drop away in three directions, but the climber's eye is immediately drawn to the jagged mass of snow and ice to the south. Sitting atop the Continental Divide, Ice Mountain and the Three Apostles almost make one stop and quickly check his map to be certain he is still in the Sawatch. The peaks' sharp ridges and deep couloirs are dramatic exceptions to normal Sawatch geography. The name "Three Apostles" refers to a group of three summits, two peaks, one of 13,570 feet to the southwest and one of 13,863 feet to the northeast, flanking the main summit, 13,920 feet, called "Ice Mountain." Here indeed is as challenging a climb as any Fourteener. While miners scoured the upper basin of the South Fork of Clear Creek and broad Harrison Flats for silver, no documented evidence of a climb of Ice Mountain existed until John L.J. Hart's climb of October 4, 1931.

THE ROUTES

South Fork Clear Creek

Four miles beyond Vicksburg (see page 93) is Winfield, which still bears a flavor of the silver boom of the 1880s thanks to the Clear Creek Canyon Historical Society. At Winfield, the north and south forks of Clear Creek meet. A dozen surrounding thir-

Huron Peak looking west from Missouri Mountain. *Gary Koontz.*

teeners and the beauty of the valley make Winfield an ideal headquarters for a week of backpacking. For Huron, hike southwest from Winfield for two miles along the South Fork to the Banker Mine, in its day a key silver producer of the valley.

A half-mile beyond the Banker, once round the west shoulder of Browns Peak, grassy slopes lead southeast to moderate talus and eventually Huron's summit. You can also continue up the valley to Hamilton. Only a few decaying logs whisper of a once bustling village whose very heartbeat relied on the cry of "Silver!" From Hamilton, a prospecting trail leads east to several old cabins (look but don't touch!) and then due east to Huron's summit.

Winfield to Summit: 4½ miles; 3,800 feet.

North Ridge

Just south of Winfield a relatively new road (not on Harvard 15M) forks left and climbs the gulch between Middle Mountain and Browns Peak. Huron can be climbed this way, but the route is less scenic and entails remaining high on the Brown-Huron ridge for the return trip, something some folks are reluctant to do in the face of approaching thunderstorms so inevitable in Colorado.

Winfield to Summit: 3 miles; 3,800 feet.

▲

Mount Harvard
14,420 feet (3rd highest)

Mount Columbia
14,073 feet (35th highest)

Mount Yale
14,196 feet (21st highest)

Mount Harvard's story begins in California in 1864. In that year, members of the California Geological Survey mapped what they thought to be the highest peak in the Sierra Nevada and named it after the Survey's director, Professor Josiah Dwight Whitney. A year later, Whitney, an 1839 graudate of Yale University, accepted a position as Professor of Geology at Harvard. In the course of his work, Whitney made plans for an expedition to the central Colorado Rockies to provide field experience for his students and particularly to obtain altitude readings of the higher peaks. His desire to explore the inner Rockies was fired by rumors, largely the result of barroom guesses by miners near Fairplay, of peaks in central Colorado exceeding 17,000 feet.

In 1869, Whitney led the first class of the Harvard Mining School, a grand total of four eager young men, and accompanying support personnel west to explore the Sawatch Range. Notable among the expedition included William H. Brewer, Whitney's assistant and a colleague from California Survey days, and Henry Gannett, in 1869, a student, but who would later gain fame with the Hayden Survey and have the highest peak in Wyoming named after him.

Whitney's party traveled west from Denver, across South Park, and into the Arkansas Valley near Trout Creek Pass. At some point between an ascent of Mount Lincoln and their descent into the Arkansas Valley, their attention focused on two prominent

Mount Columbia (right) and a portion of the Harvard-Columbia ridge from the southern slopes of Mount Harvard.

Looking north up Horn Fork Basin to Mount Harvard.

peaks of the central Sawatch. The northern summit Whitney named "Mount Harvard" after the expedition's sponsoring institution. The south summit was named "Mount Yale" after Whitney's alma mater, a christening which undoubtedly pleased Brewer, also a Yale graduate (class of 1852) and at that time Professor of Agriculture there. Whitney's action in naming the peaks after universities initiated the Collegiate Peaks section of the Sawatch.

William Brewer recorded the events of the Whitney expedition in a series of letters to his wife. Unfortunately, while flowing with general scenic description, the letters are sparse in specific geographic routes. Brewer's letters do indicate, however, that Whitney, Brewer, William M. Davis, S.F. Sharpless, and Robert Moore made the first recorded ascent of Mount Yale on August 18, 1869. A logical reading of Brewer's letters suggests that the ascent was probably from North Cottonwood Creek via some combination of the northeast ridge and the drainage of Silver Creek.

From the summit of Yale, Whitney and his companions calculated its elevation just over 14,000 feet, but observed that Mount Harvard was the higher of the two peaks. The following day, Davis and Sharpless battled rain and fog to make the first recorded ascent of Mount Harvard. Logistics with supplies and pack animals prevented Whitney and Brewer from joining them, much to Brewer's recorded chagrin. The Whitney expedition returned to Harvard certain that no 17,000-foot giants rose in the Sawatch Range and with the distinction of being the first scientific survey to penetrate the inner Colorado Rockies.

A scant four years later, Henry Gannett was back in the Sawatch Range with the Hayden Survey. Hayden's men used Mount Harvard as a triangulation station for mapping the central Sawatch.

Little attention was paid Harvard's nearest neighbor until 1916, when Roger W. Toll, who was placing Colorado Mountain Club registers on the Sawatch peaks, named it Mount Columbia. It was no small coincidence that Toll, an early pioneer of Colorado climbing, was a 1906 graduate of Columbia University. Toll went on to a notable career with the National Park Service, serving as superintendent of three national parks, Mount Rainier, Rocky Mountain, and Yellowstone.

Toll's naming of Columbia was in keeping with Whitney and

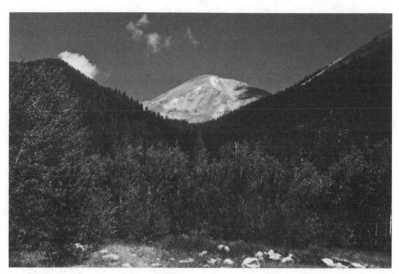

Looking north up Denny *Gulch* to Mount Yale from Collegiate Peaks Campground.

Mount Yale from the southeast slopes of its prominent sub-peak. *Gary Koontz.*

Brewer's lead, but little could any of them suspect that collegiate rivalry would reach the "heights" it did in the early 1960s. On July 13, 1962, three Harvard men, David Owen (class of '61), Henry Faulkner ('63), and Steve Potter ('62), attempted to reach the summit of Mount Harvard carrying a long metal pole topped with a sign reading: "Mt. Harvard, 14,434. This sign erected at an altitude of 14,434, making it the second highest point in the contiguous United States . . ."

While their intent to make the sign higher than Mount Elbert was obvious, approaching darkness forced the trio to cache the pole several hundred yards beneath the summit and abandon the climb. The pole and sign lay untouched until the following June when Hugh E. Kingery (Cornell, class of '54) and John and Tim Wirth (Harvard '58 and '61, respectively) chanced on the material. They lugged it the remaining distance to the summit. Kingery evidently convinced the Wirths that one Cornell man with seniority took precedence over two junior Harvard men, because Kingery was able to sign the register noting that "Cornell finished Harvard's effort today." The story, however, does not end there.

On July 11, 1963, a month after the Kingery-Wirth climb, the original Harvard lads, Owens, Faulkner, and Potter, were again in the Sawatch determined to take their pole the remaining distance to Harvard's summit. Their dismay in finding the pole gone turned to relief when they found it securely anchored in the summit rocks. Owens promptly noted a thank you in the register to the two Harvard men and the "one from Cornell, who being deprived of any Mt. Cornell, helped us make this the highest in Colorado and 2nd highest in the U.S." The entry was signed with the inspiring admonition: "Fight fiercely, Harvard!"

The pole was visible to a sharp eye from Horn Fork Basin and it remained on the summit of Harvard until sometime in the early 1980s, when it disappeared, perhaps as part of the campaign to clean up the Fourteener summits. One of the pole planters, Tim Wirth, went on to represent Colorado in the United States Senate.

With all of the Ivy League pomp and glory, the histories of Harvard and Yale have at least one episode with a homespun touch. In February of 1956, Gordon B. "Rocky" Warren, one of the pioneer pilots of the Colorado high country, was flying over the Harvard-Yale vicinity when he observed a horse stranded by deep snowdrifts on a saddle on the Continental Divide northwest of Mount Yale.

At his home base of Gunnison, Warren's report of the animal's predicament prompted Gunnison Mayor B.H. Jorgenson to provide bales of hay for the horse; Warren and fellow-pilot Ned Wallace were to drop it to the animal. On a subsequent flight, Warren took a photograph showing the horse standing contentedly over one of the bales of hay. The photograph soon focused nationwide attention on the Harvard-Yale area. The news media dubbed the horse "Elijah" after the Biblical prophet who was fed by ravens in the wilderness. Airline pilots of mountain-hopping Frontier Airlines went out of their way to show their passengers the new-found celebrity. Soon, donations for the animal's welfare were pouring into Jorgenson's office from all over the country, and Warren was able to add oats to the horse's diet.

When spring melted the snows from Elijah's timberline palace, Elijah the celebrity turned out to be none other than "Bugs," the pack horse of local residents Al and Bill Turner. Bugs was a cantankerous beast with a particular aversion to parked cars and women in skirts. Evidently, Bugs had headed to the high country to get away from it all. Just goes to show how hard it can be to get a little peace and quiet!

T H E   R O U T E S

Harvard-Columbia, Horn Fork Basin

Half the battle on this approach is finding one's way out of Buena Vista. From the town's main intersection and traffic light, where the Cottonwood Pass road and U.S. 24 intersect, drive north .4 miles on U.S. 24. Turn left (west) on Chaffee County 350 for two miles, then continue north and northwest one mile. At the Forest Service sign, "North Cottonwood Creek," turn south for .2 miles, and then continue west five miles to the end of the road and the trailhead. The road is somewhat of a washboard — what dirt side road isn't? — but it is passable in cars after it has dried out each spring. There is room to camp near the trailhead at 9,850 or lower along the road.

At the trailhead, cross the bridge to the south side of the creek and go west one and one-half miles to a trail junction just

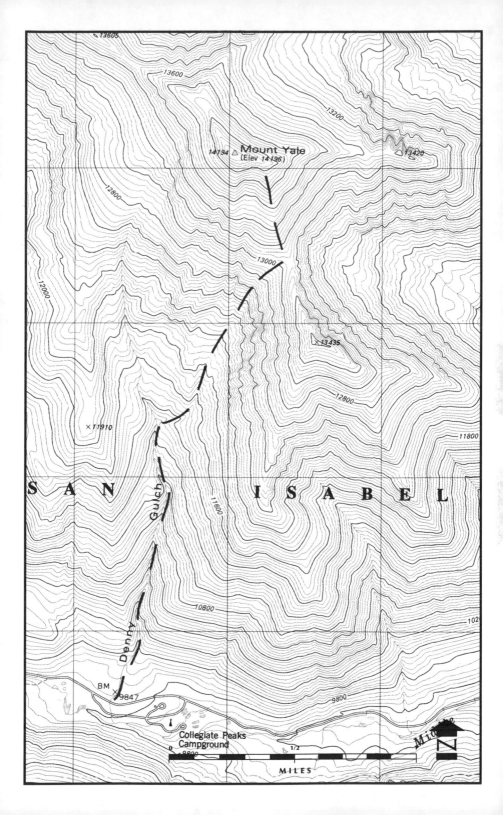

after the trail returns to the north side of the creek. The left-hand (west) trail winds to Kroenke Lake, Elijah's winter pasture, and the Continental Divide, and offers routes to Birthday Peak (12,749 feet) and the northwest shoulder of Mount Yale. The right-hand fork (north) climbs three and one-half more miles to Horn Fork Basin and Bear Lake, one of the prettiest spots in the Sawatch. A number of fine campsites can be found just below timberline as the trail enters the basin.

From the basin, Harvard dominates the view to the north while Mount Yale rises in broad Sawatch form to the south. A climb up the grassy slopes and drainages of Harvard's south shoulder and a mild scramble over the summit boulders bring you to the granite blocks on the top. If you are a ridge-runner at heart, do the Harvard-Columbia ridge. It's long, but interesting. Keep to the east side where a number of exit couloirs are available. The final towers on the ridge, dubbed "The Rabbits" even before *Watership Down*, are best skirted to the left (east) and then up the final scree slopes to Columbia's summit. To climb both peaks but avoid the ridge, drop off Harvard's southeast shoulder past the ridge (east) and up Columbia's grassy (compared to the southern scree slopes) northern slopes. For the descent of Columbia, "scree" any number of chutes west off the southern ridge. This is the normal ascent route for Columbia from Horn Fork Basin and is made far more tolerable if late spring snow remains in the couloirs to cover one of the Sawatch's more frustrating scree slopes. The Harvard-Columbia traverse from the trailhead is a long day and more enjoyable if combined with a backpack into Horn Fork Basin.

Trailhead to Harvard: 6 miles; 4,400 feet.

Trailhead to Columbia: 5 miles; 4,100 feet.

Trailhead to Harvard and Columbia: 8 miles; 5,300 feet; 5 miles on return.

Eastern Approaches

Harvard and Columbia can also be reached from the Harvard Trail up Frenchman Creek which leaves U.S. 24 at Riverside, seven miles north of Buena Vista and from Pine Creek Trail which leaves U.S. 24 about 12 miles north of Buena Vista. The latter route offers a number of backpacking possibilities in Missouri Basin.

Mount Yale, Middle Cottonwood Creek

Mount Yale is considered by some to be the best one-day "family" climb in the Sawatch. It still requires almost 4,400 feet of elevation gain, however, and there are some users of the first edition who have refuted that description. Remember, of course, that unless you drive part way up Princeton, all of the Sawatch climbs require big elevation gains. From Buena Vista's main intersection, drive west on the Cottonwood Pass road, Colorado 306, for 11 miles to Collegiate Peaks campground. Three-tenths of a mile west of the main entrance to the campground, a dirt road leads north up Denny Gulch. Mount Yale is easily visible at the head of the gulch. Be certain you are in Denny GULCH; more than one would-be Yale climber has taken Denny CREEK where a large traihead is located and wound up having to bushwhack up Delaney Gulch and Yale's west face, if he made the summit at all. The Denny Gulch road soon becomes a trail which winds up the gulch through fallen timber. The gulch is a rainbow of wildflowers in late July and August.

At 11,300 feet, where Denny Gulch splits, take the right-hand fork (east) and pick your way to the saddle south of the summit, plainly visible. Any attempt to climb east out of the gulch sooner sends one up Yale's infamous sub-peak (13,440). From the saddle, continue north up the ridge to the summit. This route avoids the long climb over the sub-peak which is necessary on the popular winter routes of either of two prominent couloirs between Harris Gulch and Denny Gulch. In winter, however, exceptionally good glissades make the labor worthwhile.

Collegiate Peaks Campground to Summit: 3 miles; 4,400 feet.

The east ridge of Yale also offers a moderate climb from the Main Range Trail. Pick up the Main Range Trail either on North or Middle Cottonwood creeks and follow it until it crosses Yale's east ridge at 11,800 feet; from there, it's a two-mile climb west along the ridge to the summit.

Middle Cottonwood Creek to Summit: 4½ miles, 4,800 feet.
North Cottonwood Creek to Summit: 4½ miles, 4,800 feet.

▲

Mount Princeton

14,197 feet (18th highest)

The southernmost of the Collegiate Peaks, Mount Princeton rises in grand majesty with a graceful symmetry quite unique among Colorado's Fourteeners. Seen from the east, the peak presents three summits, with the two lower ones flanking the highest central peak in almost-perfect balance. Mount Princeton is considered by many to be the most attractive of the Sawatch peaks as seen from the Arkansas Valley, and in many ways is symbolic of the Colorado Rockies as a whole — dramatic in its abrupt rise from the valley floor, yet attractive in form and rich in legends and history of surveys, mining, and tourists.

The south slope of Mount Princeton drops off abruptly in an escarpment known as the Chalk Cliffs. In reality, the cliffs are not chalk at all, but are composed of white quartz monzonite in a crumbling state, thereby giving the early visitors the impression of being chalk. These striking cliffs have long been a prominent feature of Mount Princeton and have given rise to at least one legend concerning lost Spanish treasure. This legend purports that approximately 200 years ago, a small group of Spaniards from settlements in New Mexico raided an Indian village and escaped with a large amount of valuable items. The Indians quickly pursued the thieves, and the Spaniards were forced to stash the treasure somewhere in the Chalk Cliffs. The treasure achieved its "lost" status when the Indians caught up with the raiders and killed them, but could not locate their stolen goods. The search has continued for 200 years, but the treasure will probably remain lost forever among the dangerous cliffs, if it even exists.

The white cliffs also inspired the Wheeler Survey to give the peak its original name, "Chalk Mountain." However, Mount Princeton is found in use as early as 1873, and it is suspected that this name was given by Henry Gannett of the Hayden Survey, in keeping with the other nearby Collegiate Peaks. It is not recorded that either members of the Hayden or Wheeler surveys ascended Mount Princeton, but it is a possibility.

Mount Princeton from the east, above the Arkansas River Valley.

The first recorded climb of Mount Princeton was accomplished in 1877 by William Libbey, Jr., of Princeton University. Libbey had just received his degree, and he accompanied other students and a professor on what amounted to a practicum in scientific study and surveying in the mountains of Colorado and Utah. Mount Princeton proved to be an irresistable goal for obvious reasons, and on July 17, 1877, William Libbey reached the summit on a solo ascent. Appropriately, Libbey later became a professor of geography at Princeton, and no doubt he enjoyed retelling many times of the day he conquered the mountain which bears the name of his alma mater.

The possibility that Princeton was first ascended by miners is supported by the fact that the Hortense Mine was discovered at about 12,000 feet on the southern peak of Mount Princeton in July of 1872 by J. A. Merriam and E. W. Keyes. The Hortense became one of the finest silver-producers of the Sawatch Range, but access was extremely difficult over a narrow, twisting, ledge trail. However, the mine was producing $100 per ton of ore, and such a figure was ample incentive for the new manager, Eugene

Teats, to construct a five-mile wagon road. Before long, the burro pack trains were replaced by oxen-drawn wagons, and this improvement enabled the Hortense to operate profitably for many years until the ore finally played out.

Most of the miners who worked at the Hortense commuted from residences at the southeast foot of Mount Princeton. This settlement centered around a group of seven hot springs which had been known to the Utes long before the miners entered the area. It was inevitable that the hot springs would be commercially developed, for in the latter part of the 1800s, Colorado was developing a reputation as a health spa paradise. By 1884, the Mount Princeton Hot Springs were sporting a newly completed hotel, but due to financial problems and the fading of the Chalk Creek boom towns, no paying guests were received for a number of years. Finally, the property changed hands in 1915, and it blossomed into a first-class resort. When completed, the hotel had 100 rooms, stained glass windows, and a huge ballroom. In addition to the hot springs, other outdoor facilities included tennis courts and a nine-hole golf course, undoubtedly one of the highest in the nation at that time.

Mount Princeton Hot Springs flourished for about 15 years, with high-class guests arriving in glistening chauffered Cadillacs from the train depot at Buena Vista. The bubble burst, however, with the great crash in 1929. In the 1930s, the property was renamed the Antero Hotel, but it led a struggling existence until finally the grand building was razed in 1950. The hot springs still survive, however, and are receiving somewhat of a revival in business today.

T H E   R O U T E S

Mount Princeton Hot Springs

Mount Princeton is one Fourteener which very inconsiderately is located on the corner of four adjoining 15M quads. Be that as it may, drive south on U.S. 285 from Buena Vista for eight miles to Colorado 162 and west four miles to the site of famed Mount Princeton Hot Springs, then north on Chaffee County 321 for about one mile to the upper area of Young Life's Frontier Camp. From here, the prominent southeast ridge with the broad

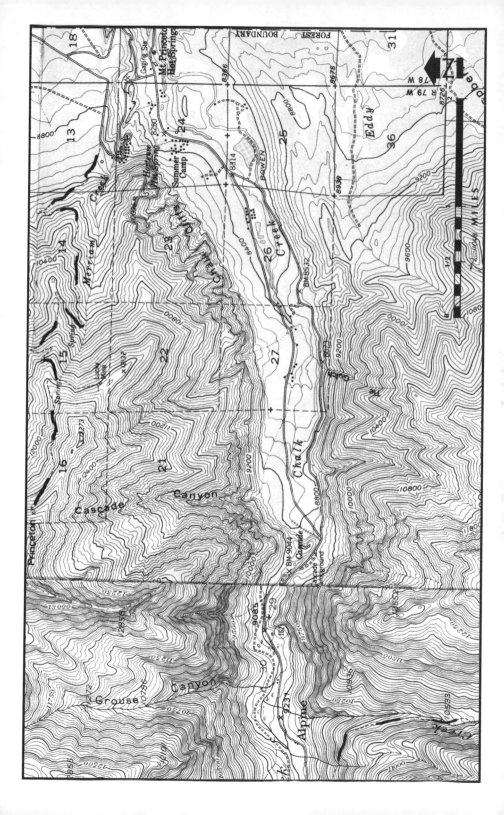

couloir may be reached via a direct assault up Merriam Creek or following a switchbacking jeep road four miles to the site of a chalet maintained by the ranch. Just north of the chalet at the Merrian Creek drainage, a trail of sorts leads west, skirting the sub-peak of the southeast ridge, past the ruins of the Hortense Mine, and on two miles to the summit.

Frontier Camp to Summit direct: 3½ miles; 5,400 feet.

▲

Mount Antero

14,269 feet (10th highest)

No Colorado Fourteener, not even any of the mineral-rich peaks of the Mosquitoes, can come close to matching the wealth of gems which Mount Antero has produced. Many a Fourteener can claim one or two great mines on its flanks which have produced fabulous amounts of gold or silver, but Mount Antero has cornered the market on aquamarine, topaz, and clear and smoky quartz crystals.

Mount Antero rises south of Mount Princeton, across Chalk Creek, which was the scene of extensive mining activity during the 1870s, and it was probably climbed by prospectors during this time, but the specifics of any first ascent have not been recorded. While these early silver prospectors may have noticed Mount Antero's rich gem field, they staked no claims on it and made no mention of the gems.

Part of the reason for the neglect of Mount Antero's gems was the discovery of a number of promising silver mines in the area, mainly to the west of Mount Antero. These discoveries lured hopeful prospectors into the Chalk Creek Valley, and in 1879 the community of Alpine was incorporated, located directly below Mount Antero's northwest flank. In many ways, Alpine was a classic mining camp, with about 1,000 people, its own newspaper (the *True Fissure*), three banks, two hotels, no church, but 23 saloons. Alpine's earliest and principal silver mine was the Tilden, which was located on the slopes of Boulder Mountain, just west of Mount Antero.

Alpine was the major supply point for the area and a booming town with a bright future until 1881, when the Denver, South Park and Pacific Railroad arrived in the Chalk Creek Valley. The narrow gauge rails pushed rapidly through Alpine, and soon reached the rival town of St. Elmo, about five miles up the valley. This was just what struggling St. Elmo needed, and the population skyrocketed, drawing many of its residents from Alpine. As a result, by 1882, Alpine was little more than a memory, providing a classic history of a short-lived but rip-roaring mining camp of

Looking west to Mount Antero from the Arkansas Valley.

the Colorado Rockies. Today, a few summer homes mark the site of Alpine, but St. Elmo is a superbly preserved ghost town, thus outdoing its former rival even today.

As Alpine faded and St. Elmo blossomed, a lone prospector by the name of Nathaniel D. Wanemaker combed the slopes of Mount Antero, far above the bustling activity of the valley. Wanemaker had forgotten about silver prospecting in the Sawatch, ever since he had discovered crystals of blue aquamarine high on the mountain in 1884. Wanemaker soon realized the great potential in mining Antero's gems, and proceeded to construct a small stone cabin at about 13,400 feet on the south side of the peak. Reportedly, he found $600 worth of gems his first year on Antero, and lived on the mountain many years thereafter, singlehandedly collecting what gems he could find.

Wanemaker's discovery attracted many others to the peak,

and in the years that followed, a number of impressive finds were made, both by professional prospectors and amateur rockhounds. The most popular of Antero's gems was the aquamarine, which ranged from pale blue-green to deep blue in color. Many of the better aquamarine specimens were sent to Germany to be cut into jewelry-quality gems and then returned to the United States. In addition, Mount Antero has yielded huge clear quartz crystals, including a seven-inch one which is currently located in the Harvard Mineralogical Museum. One of the largest clear quartz crystals from Mount Antero was shaped into a crystal sphere nearly six inches in diameter and displayed at the 1893 Columbian Exposition. Smoky quartz is more common than clear quartz on the mountain, with some specimens weighing as much as 50 pounds.

Recognizing the value of Mount Antero as a mineral site, the Colorado Mineralogical Society held ceremonies on the peak on August 1, 1949, creating the Mount Antero Mineral Park. A bronze tablet was placed in a granite boulder near the summit of the peak, officially making Mount Antero the highest mineral locality in North America. Recently, the only commercial mining on the mountain has been for beryllium, and this activity was responsible for the construction of a road to 13,500 feet on Mount Antero's south shoulder in the 1950s. Gem hunting among amateur rockhounds still remains popular on the peak, and while most of the best mineral specimens have been removed from Antero, the watchful mountaineer may still be able to find a good specimen of light blue aquamarine or clear quartz.

Mount Antero was named for Chief Antero of the Uintah band of the Ute Indians. The situation surrounding the naming of the peak is somewhat obscure, for while the name is given in the 1879 atlas of the Hayden Survey, it is not mentioned in any of the Hayden reports. As a Uintah chief, Antero spent most of his time in Utah, but he was one of the chiefs to sign an 1878 treaty which ceded portions of Ute land in the San Juans to the silver-hungry white men. In addition, Chief Antero helped to quell an uprising of another band of Utes in 1867, and he kept his own band peaceful during the White River Utes' uprising in 1879. John Jerome Hart suggests that Antero's peaceful cooperation with the whites at that time may have been responsible for naming the peak for him.

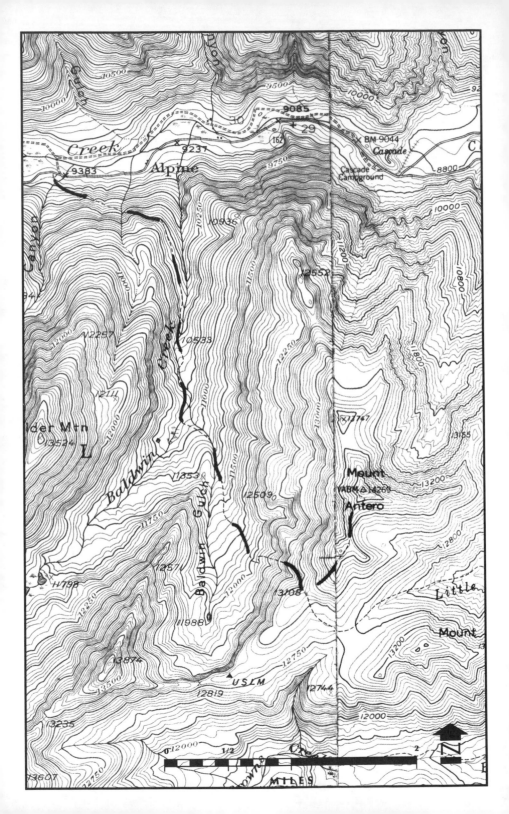

T H E   R O U T E S

Baldwin Gulch

From Buena Vista, drive south on U.S. 285 for eight miles, then west on Colorado 162 about twelve and one-half miles to just west of the old site of Alpine where the Baldwin Gulch road enters from the south (9,383 feet). Turn left (south) and climb a rocky jeep road two and one-half miles into Baldwin Gulch to a fork in the road and creek crossing. Follow the trail across the creek to its end on Antero's south shoulder near the gem mine at 13,500 feet. Climbing directly east from the creek crossing only takes you onto one of the most "mobile" talus slopes of the Sawatch. From the mine, the summit is a half-mile north along the ridge.

Baldwin Gulch Creek crossing to Summit: 3½ miles; 3,300 feet.

A winter approach to Antero may be made from just east of Cascade Campground on Colorado 162, nine miles west of U.S. 285. A prominent, treeless couloir climbs to the north ridge and then over a sub-peak to the summit. The adventuresome climber should try Antero from the south, starting from Shavano Campground (see Tabeguache and Shavano), climbing Tabeguache and Shavano, backtracking over Tabeguache, crossing Brown's Creek Basin, climbing Antero from the gem mine, and then descending Baldwin Gulch to Chalk Creek, where hopefully a ride is waiting. It's an 18-mile, 8,700-vertical day, recommended only for the superbly conditioned.

▲

Mount Shavano

14,229 feet (17th highest)

Tabeguache Mountain

14,155 feet (26th highest)

Mount Shavano and Tabeguache Mountain are two of only four Colorado Fourteeners which bear names of Indian origin. Appropriately, Shavano was a prominent chief of the Tabeguache branch of the Utes, and to add even more Indian character to the peaks, a number of Ute legends have been born concerning a mysterious snow formation which appears on the east flank of Mount Shavano each spring. However, like much of the West, the Indian heritage remains in name and legend only. The Indians themselves were forced from the area by miners in the 1870s, who brought more permanent "civilization" to the area and left their marks upon the peaks.

Chief Shavano was prominent among Ute leaders, and therefore was often an important figure in Indian-white relations. He first gained favor with the whites when he helped to capture Kaneache, another Ute who began a small-scale rebellion in 1867. In 1873, Shavano was among 133 Utes who signed the Brunot Treaty which ceded most of the San Juans to the whites. Trespassing violations by miners took Shavano and others to Washington, D.C., for negotiations, and finally, in 1878, Shavano, Ouray, Antero, and others signed a second treaty which settled the problem in favor of the miners. Shavano continued to demonstrate loyalty to the whites when he helped to rescue the white women captured by the White River Utes following the Meeker Massacre in 1879. For all of his efforts, Shavano was favored by Chief Ouray as a possible successor to himself, but after Ouray's death in 1880, political manipulations prevented Shavano from taking the position; five years later, he also died.

Shavano's name as applied to the mountain appears on maps as early as 1875, indicating his popularity with the whites at that

Summit of Tabeguache Mountain from the west ridge. Mount Shavano's summit visible behind and to the right. *R. Omar Richardson.*

Mount Shavano and angel from southeast. *Colorado Historical Society.*

time. However, the Wheeler Survey named the mountain "Usher Peak," after Judge J. P. Usher, Chief Counsel for the Denver and Rio Grande Railway, but his name never gained acceptance. Tabeguache Mountain was recognized as being more than 14,000 feet as early as 1913, but it was not named or recognized as a separate peak from Mount Shavano until 1931, when the Colorado Mountain Club officially recognized it as such.

Mount Shavano and Indian legends are inseparable, for each spring a figure of snow with upstretched arms, known as the Angel of Shavano, appears on the eastern flank of the mountain. Like the Holy Cross, this formation has bred a multitude of legends. It is virtually impossible to determine which of these legends is of the greatest antiquity, or which are even genuinely Indian in origin.

Numerous legends concerning the alleviation of drought reflect natural associations with a snow formation which produces precious life-giving water. One legend says that long ago a severe drought was forcing the Indians from the area. As a last resort before leaving, an Indian princess knelt at the foot of Mount Shavano and prayed for rain. The Indian god to whom she prayed demanded that she sacrifice herself for the sake of her tribe. She did so, and every year thereafter, the princess appears as the Angel of Shavano. The Angel weeps for her people, and her tears in the form of melting snow, symbolic of her sacrifice, provide the valuable moisture to the land below.

Another legend, obviously of relatively recent origin, is of interest because it involves Chief Shavano himself and the great Black scout, Jim Beckwourth. This legend contends that Shavano and Beckwourth were close friends, and when Beckwourth was fatally injured in 1853, Shavano went to the mountain to pray for Beckwourth's soul. Each spring afterward, the Angel appears to indicate that Shavano's prayers have indeed been answered.

Mining activity in the vicinity of Shavano and Tabeguache dates as early as 1863, when a few gold seekers staked claims on the eastern side of Mount Shavano. These claims never amounted to much, but in the 1870s, better finds of gold were made to the west and south of Tabeguache Mountain. In 1879, a mining camp sprang up at 11,000 feet at the southwest foot of Tabeguache Mountain, and it was christened "Clifton." Before long, it was renamed "Shavano," and by 1880, the camp held about 100 people.

Over the years, Shavano had three general stores, three mills, but only one saloon. As mining camps went, Shavano was quite placid, experiencing only one murder and one hanging, both revolving around the same incident. Apparently, the mining activity around Shavano was quite placid as well, for the town lasted only about three years. In the years that followed, a few individual mines continued to operate, but after 1907, Shavano proper was never inhabited. Some prospecting continued, and in 1913, the Shavano Mining and Milling Company was busy drilling a tunnel at 13,400 feet on the south shoulder of Mount Shavano. The tunnel was cut into a lead which had been opened on the surface in the saddle above, and which had yielded $40 per ton in gold. The mine was never profitable, but the remains of the workings are still clearly evident in Mount Shavano's broad south saddle.

Shavano and Tabeguache were probably first scaled by miners, but one climb in 1888 by Charles Fay had widespread publicity through the magazine *Appalachia*. Fay climbed Mount Shavano, hardly a noteworthy mountaineering landmark, but the readers of *Appalachia* devoured any sort of outdoor adventure, and the fact that Fay began climbing at 2:30 A.M. gave his account some added dramatic appeal.

Barely missing the 14,000-foot mark is Mount Ouray at 13,971 feet, located approximately 14 miles south of Mount Shavano. While not a Fourteener, the massive cone of Mount Ouray is nonetheless impressive enough to easily deserve the name of the great Ute chief. No one man did more to preserve peace between the Utes and the whites than Chief Ouray.

While Mount Ouray is not rich in mining history, it is closely tied with narrow-gauge railroad history. Marshall Pass, at 10,846 feet, is located on the southern flank of the peak and is the lowest crossing of the Sawatch Range. Discovered in 1873 by William Marshall, the pass became a route for one of Otto Mears' toll roads in 1879, and then was occupied by Palmer's Denver and Rio Grande Railway in 1881. The pass proved to be the best railroad route into the Gunnison country, and for more than 70 years, the Marshall Pass line was a featured part of "The Scenic Line of the World."

T H E   R O U T E S

Tabeguache and Shavano, Jennings Creek

AVOID MCCOY GULCH! AVOID MCCOY GULCH!! AVOID MCCOY GULCH!!! No route in the first edition caused us more consternation than this one! We recommended a route up Jennings Creek and over Tabeguache to Shavano, specifically warning against McCoy Gulch. Despite this, some parties returning from Shavano have been suckered into descending easy-looking McCoy Gulch. Out of sight from above, McCoy Gulch is blocked by steep cliffs and a maze of downed timber. Numerous search and rescue operations have plucked unprepared and uninformed hikers from McCoy's cliffs. There is now a fairly well-established trail up Tabeguache's south ridge from Jennings Creek and one dropping west from the saddle south of Shavano. This allows you to traverse upper McCoy Gulch and skirt Tabeguache on the return from Shavano, but you must still remember to exit the gulch before dropping too low. Popular use to the contrary, we continue to describe our original route, which, if followed, will keep you entirely clear of McCoy Gulch.

From Maysville, west of Poncha Springs on U.S. 50, take the North Fork road north northwest for eight miles to Jennings Creek at 10,500 feet. Climb north up Jennings Creek almost to the head of the gulch and angle east (right) to the broad end of Tabeguache's west ridge. Follow the ridge with several scrambling cuts, east one mile to the summit. Shavano is one mile east and southeast, via an easy ridge with a 400-foot drop. Return via the same route; DO NOT descend McCoy Gulch.

Jennings Creek crossing to Tabeguache: 3 miles; 3,600 feet.

Jennings Creek crossing to Tabeguache and Shavano; 4 miles; 4,100 feet with 400 feet on the return over Tabeguache.

Mount Shavano Southeast Couloir

A more direct route to Shavano is available for winter ascents. From Maysville, drive almost four miles up the North Fork road to about 9,200. As the road swings west, a prominent couloir dominates the southeast flank of Shavano. This couloir is in line with the 13,611-foot sub-peak south of Shavano's summit. Climb the eastern ridge of this steep couloir to the sub-peak. The cone of Shavano's summit is one mile to the north and 800 feet above

the 13,400-foot broad saddle. The final 800 feet to the summit is easy talus hopping unless the wind is blowing a steady 55 mph with gusts to 70 mph as it was on one March ascent by the authors. From Shavano's summit, Tabeguache may be climbed via the ridge described above. The return is via the ascent route with the possibility of a glissade down the southeast couloir if avalanche conditions permit.

Foot of couloir to Shavano: 3 miles; 5,200 feet.

Foot of couloir to Shavano and Tabeguache: 4 miles; 5,600 feet, with 500 feet on return over Shavano.

▲

Red, Rugged, and Rotten: The Elk Range

For many, the epitome of Colorado mountain grandeur lies in the heart of the Elk Range, the Maroon Bells. Indeed, few Colorado sights can match the combination of colors presented by the Maroon Bells flanked with stands of flaming golden aspen and set against a crystalline blue sky, but the Elk Range is far more than the Maroon Bells. Many other peaks share the unusual red-layered nature of the Bells, while the thin, sweeping ridges of Capitol and Snowmass peaks provide mountain beauty of another sort. In addition, winter transforms the Elk Range into an incredible collection of snow-frosted peaks which appear to be taken directly from a Christmas card. The beauty of the Elk Range, regardless of the season, and the unmatched quality of its light powder snow have made it one of the nation's foremost recreation areas.

The Elk Range is one of the smallest ranges in the state, only about 45 miles long and 30 miles wide. Topographically, it is connected to the Sawatch Range to the southeast. It lies on the western side of the Continental Divide; it is drained on the north by the Roaring Fork and Crystal rivers, and on the south by the East and Taylor rivers, tributaries of the Gunnison. The valleys of the Elk Range are generally steep-sided and narrow, and the rule for the higher elevations of the range is ruggedness. Only one of the six Fourteeners of the range has a walk-up route to the summit, and even the passes are high and rugged. No regular automobile road has dared venture across the southern crest of the range, and those passes which do exist connecting with the Gunnison country, such as Schofield, Pearl, and Taylor, are occupied only by jeep or foot trails and are legendary for their toughness.

At the heart of the beauty of the Elk Range is its geology. Unlike most Colorado ranges which are predominantly of Precambrian igneous rock, the Elk Range displays Paleozoic sedimentaries on many of its peaks. During the last part of the Paleozoic Era, the area of the Elks was apparently part of a large mud flat and delta which accumulated sediments eroded from the surrounding uplands. Eventually, sediments from this erosion reached thicknesses of as much as 10,000 feet; these were compacted and metamorphosed into what is called the Maroon Formation. It is this formation which composes the greater portion of the Maroon Bells, Castle Peak, and Pyramid Peak.

During the Laramide Orogeny, the sedimentary rocks of the former mud flat were greatly uplifted in association with the uplift of the Sawatch Anticline to the east. This caused the layers of the sedimentary rocks to be tilted at an angle, and in some places, thrust over one another. As a result, today the general angle of the sedimentary rocks in the Elks slopes upward to the east. During and after uplift, igneous intrusions invaded parts of the Elks, and this activity explains why sedimentary peaks rise virtually next door to igneous peaks. The Snowmass Stock is the largest of these intrusions; it contains the granite rock, granodiorite, which composes Snowmass and Capitol peaks.

As in all other Colorado ranges, glaciation made great changes in the Elk Range. Large glaciers formed in the higher valleys and ground away at the slopes of peaks to leave the narrow and beautiful ridges of the Snowmass-Capitol area as well as the classic glacial lakes in the Pierre Lakes Basin. The upper Roaring Fork Valley remains a characteristically U-shaped glacial valley.

E. G. Beckwith named the Elk Range when he saw it from a distance in 1853, but in 1874, Henry Gannett made note that until the surveys, the Elk Range was "as little known as any part of the western territories." Both Hayden and Wheeler survey teams entered the Elks in 1873 and were deeply impressed by its unique and complex geology and unmatched beauty. Castle and Snowmass were the only two Fourteeners ascended by the Hayden Survey, while the Wheeler men climbed no peaks above 14,000 feet.

After the Leadville silver boom of the late 1870s, prospectors filtered across the Sawatch Range via Independence Pass to search for similar lodes. By 1879, four small mining camps had been established in the Elk Range, including Ute City, which became Aspen the following year. An incredible amount of high-grade silver ore was found on the hillsides south of town, and when Independence Pass was improved to wagon-road status in 1881, Aspen's boom was on. By 1889, the area had produced approximately $10 million, and Aspen's population was more than 8,000.

By the early 1900s, the silver mines of the Elk Range operated only sporadically, and it appeared that the area would never regain the economic status it had enjoyed in the 1880s. During World War II, however, ski troopers from Camp Hale, near Tennessee Pass, skied the hills near Aspen and became intrigued with the idea of developing a downhill ski area. By the late 1940s, the fame of Aspen's deep powder snows was beginning to spread — and the rest is history.

Castle Peak

14,265 feet (12th highest)

The highest mountain in the Elk Range, Castle Peak dominates the upper reaches of the Castle Creek Valley. Somewhat
isolated, the peak is seldom seen by the casual traveler, but the
hiker and climber who venture into its vicinity are rewarded with
splendid views of its rich coloration and pinnacled ridges. While
the peak is not well known today, it was familiar to many miners
of the 1880s, and no Fourteener in the Elk Range can match the
rich mining history of Castle Peak.

Although one may walk to the summit of Castle relatively
easily if the right route is taken, it was doubtful that the peak
was climbed until 1873 when the Hayden Survey passed through
the Elk Range. Members of the party were impressed with the
numerous rock towers and spires along the peak's south ridge,
and the descriptive name was born. Realizing that Castle Peak
was probably the highest summit in the Elks, they chose to climb
it, but from the difficult south side. The party began their climb
from a timberline camp southwest of the peak and were soon
confronted with several bands of small cliffs. Henry Gannett
related in a 1902 article in *Everybody's Magazine* that they made
their way through the cliffs via a series of chimneys in which
they used a counterforce technique involving climbing with their
backs and feet on opposite sides of the chimney — quite an
advanced climbing technique for 1873! Gannett and his partners
found the ridge they gained to be extremely narrow in places,
so much so that they sometimes had to straddle it and move
along in a sitting position. Finally, however, the team reached
the top, and they can almost surely be credited with a first ascent
as well as having completed what may have been the most
technically difficult climb made in the Rocky Mountains until
that time. Not surprisingly, Gannett reported that Castle "afforded
more of a climb than any other Colorado mountain with which
I have any acquaintance."

By 1880, a small mining camp had grown up about 12 miles

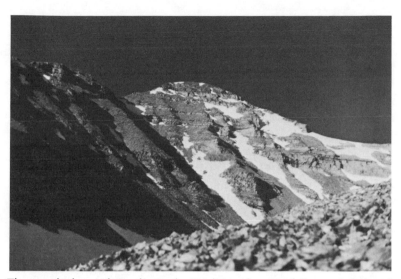

The north face of Castle Peak. Traditional route follows right-hand skyline. *Gary Koontz.*

up Castle Creek from Aspen, known as Castle Forks City. In January of 1882, it became known as Ashcroft, but did not appear to have much of a future as a silver camp. In the spring of 1882, however, the Fitzgerald brothers and Jake Sands found rich silver ore in the Montezuma Mine, at 12,700 feet in the basin on Castle's northeast flank. Immediately there was quite a legal battle for the rights to the mine. Eventually it ended up in the hands of none other than H. A. W. Tabor of Leadville.

The rich strikes at the Montezuma and the Tam O'Shanter Mine, also owned by Tabor, caused Ashcroft to boom, and it grew from 500 to 2,000 in one year's span. In time, a mill and aerial tram were built to serve the Montezuma Mine. Even though the two mines produced up to $20,000 a month, Tabor poured more money into them than he ever received, and the 1893 silver crash spelled final doom for the operations. By 1900, the Montezuma had virtually ceased operation, and today only scattered remains of the mine and mill survive to remind the hiker and mountaineer of the once promising business venture. The town of Ashcroft lives again today, thanks to the restoration efforts of the U.S. Forest Service, the Aspen Historical Society, and numerous others.

T H E   R O U T E S

Montezuma Basin

From Aspen, drive northwest a half-mile on Colorado 82 to the junction of the Ashcroft and Maroon Lake roads. Turn left and then immediately take the left-hand fork which leads up Castle Creek. Drive 11.5 miles to Ashcroft and then 1.5 miles farther to a fork where the main road continues up the valley toward mining operations and the right-hand (west) fork climbs southwest into a stand of aspens, which provides a good campsite.

Hike southwest along the road from the campsite for about two and one-half miles past the site of the old Montezuma Mill, across the creek, and to the junction of the road to Pearl Pass (11,100 feet). Take the right-hand fork and proceed another one and one-half miles into the flats in the basin. From the basin, two routes are possible, either via Castle's northeast ridge or via the bowl directly northwest of this ridge. For the ridge, continue up the valley a quarter-mile to about 12,400 feet, about a quarter-mile south of the Montezuma Mine. Climb southwest up the shallow gully on the northeast ridge which leads to the visible false summit of Castle (13,760 feet). The northeast ridge can also be reached by continuing into the bowl described below and then angling south onto the ridge. From the false summit, it is another three-eights of a mile southwest along the ridge to the summit.

The bowl route, which is not so steep, leaves the road at about 12,400 feet, almost to the Montezuma Mine. Continue west up the main drainage a half-mile and then follow it southwest another half-mile into the bowl. Scramble southwest to the low point in Castle's northwest ridge (13,800 feet). Continue up the ridge a quarter-mile southeast to the summit. From the saddle, you may want to make the side trip a quarter-mile northwest to the subsidiary summit of 14,022-foot Conundrum, one of those points above 14,000 feet which has not officially been verified as a separate Fourteener. From the summit of Castle, a good but steep glissade may be found off a north-face couloir and into the

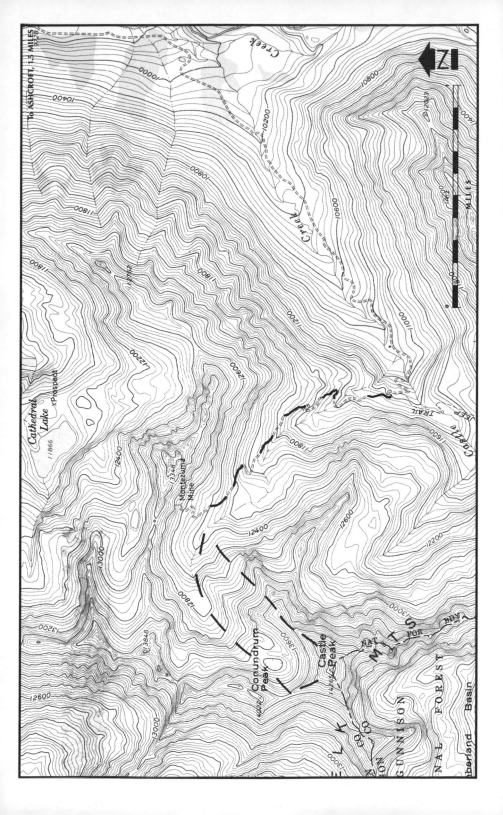

bowl, or descent may be made by either of the above-described ascent routes.

Castle Creek campsite (9,900 feet) to Summit (either route): 5 miles; 4,400 feet (excluding Conundrum).

▲

Pyramid Peak
14,018 feet (47th highest)

Driving south from Aspen toward Maroon Lake, many an expectant eye, eagerly awaiting the Maroon Bells, is first treated to the towering mass of crumbling spires dominating the valley above the confluence of East and West Maroon creeks. To be sure, its rugged symmetry deserves the name "Pyramid."

In general, the surveyors of the Hayden and Wheeler surveys kept their distance from the crumbling walls of Pyramid and the Maroons. Wheeler's eminent geologist, Professor John Stevenson did, however, report an ascent by the team's topographer, a man named Young, to within several hundred feet of a peak which could easily have been either Pyramid or North Maroon, from Stevenson's description. While some sources credit Young with the first near-miss on Pyramid, the writers conclude that Young ascended to near the top of North Maroon. There is ample room for discussion, and folks wishing to draw their own conclusion should consult *Roof of the Rockies* for Stevenson's description.

Regardless of Young's exploits, the first complete ascent of Pyramid appears to have been the August 31, 1909, climb of Percy Hagerman and Harold Clark. Hagerman was the son of J. J. Hagerman, entrepreneur-extraordinaire of the Colorado Midland Railroad and Hagerman Tunnel fame. Percy followed in his father's footsteps and developed a number of business and mining interests. Harold Clark was a prominent Aspen lawyer who also had a number of mining interests. Busy as they were in their individual pursuits, Hagerman and Clark teamed together during the summers of 1908, 1909, and 1910 to climb virtually every major summit in the Elks. Hagerman was 39 in 1908, and Clark was 46, no young ages for accomplishing feats which must rank with Dwight Lavender and Mel Griffith's pioneering of the San Juans. Hagerman Peak near Snowmass Peak, and Clark Peak east of Capitol were named for the climbers.

Hagerman and Clark's climbing legacy became "Notes on Mountaineering in the Elk Mountains," which Hagerman com-

Pyramid Peak from Buckskin Pass looking east. The route climbs into the large amphitheater with the patch of snow and then diverts either left to the north ridge or right to the west-face "couloir and ledges" approach as described. *Glen Gebhardt.*

piled in 1912. In it, Hagerman stressed a fact well known to later Pyramid climbers — the loose rock hazards of the mountain, particularly in the chimneys and couloirs.

A route on Pyramid's crumbling, 1,800-foot north face was pioneered in June of 1952, by a team led by Harvey Carter. The first winter ascent of the peak was made in February 1969 by Gordon Whitmer and Fritz Stammberger.

THE ROUTES

Pyramid must rank as one of the toughest of Colorado's Fourteeners on anyone's list because of technical difficulties, loose-rock hazard, and the fact that the mountain is a very complex network of couloirs and ridges. A wrong turn on Pyramid does not bring one to a broad, grassy, "Oh-well-we'll-go-down-this-way" slope — rather, to a frequently hazardous situation.

From the parking lot at Maroon Lake (see Maroon Peak), hike up the trail toward Crater Lake for almost one mile to an area of downed timber and rock where an increasingly used trail wanders southeast across the drainage from Crater Lake and then south up the prominent couloir that drains the huge amphitheater of Pyramid's north side. After one mile of steep climbing into the amphitheater, contour south (right) around the amphitheater bowl to the low point of the ridge running from Pyramid's summit to a small western sub-peak. Pass southwest across the ridge at about 12,700 feet and work immediately east across ledges and then up a long, narrow couloir full of loose and sliding rock. The couloir ends abruptly beneath a large rock face to the south (right of the couloir exit). To the east, the view drops off into the many couloirs circling the amphitheater. Climb south up the rock steps. Party members unfamiliar with the joys (?) of exposure may wish a rope here. Keep to the west of the main summit buttress. Continue south across a series of ledges, exposed and tricky if snow covered, then east up another section of rock face, but with a good crack, to finish on the peak's south ridge a hundred feet below the summit.

For the descent, follow the north ridge around the amphitheater until a shallow couloir gives exit from the ridge to the amphitheater, at about 13,000 feet. The ridge is loose and includes at least one relatively exposed down-climb section, but is generally less exposed than the western route. Once in the amphitheater, return to Crater Lake Trail via the exit couloir from the amphitheater. Climbers may wish to ascend via the descent route described or make a round-trip climb via one route.

Maroon Lake to Summit and return with traverse as described: 6 miles; 4,400 feet.

▲

Maroon Peak

14,156 feet (25th highest)

North Maroon Peak

14,014 feet (50th highest)

Immortalized on seemingly countless calendars, placemats, notecards, and other assorted memorabilia, for many tourists the Maroon Bells *are* Colorado. To be sure, it is the Bells' popularity and easy access more than their technical difficulties which have led inexperienced parties into trouble and earned the peaks the name "The Deadly Bells." A combination of poor rock, complex routes, and bad weather has also spelled disaster for the most competent of parties. Tourists and mystique aside, the Maroon Bells are without a doubt two of the most picturesque of Colorado's high peaks and two of the most difficult Fourteeners to climb.

The Hayden and Wheeler surveys mapped and admired the Bells, but did not reach their summits. It is possible, however, that one member of the Wheeler Survey did come within several hundred feet of the summit of North Maroon, a climb which some have reported to be an early attempt on Pyramid (see Pyramid). The Hayden men correctly named the Bells formation "Maroon Mountain" and regarded the North Bell as merely a sub-peak. Later usage prompted a change to "Maroon Peak" in an attempt to identify two distinct summits. Indeed, it seems that counting the Bells as two distinct Fourteeners stems far more from their popularity than geography. The maximum drop from the north Bell to the saddle separating it from the peak is only 234 feet in a total distance of 2,100 feet.

Hart and Bueler speculate on a possible ascent of Maroon Peak by a local boy in the 1890s, but the first documented ascent of the peak came on August 28, 1908, when Percy Hagerman (see Pyramid) reached the summit solo via the south ridge. This

The Maroon Bells in April, from the northeast on the approach to Crater Lake. *Lyndon J. Lampert.*

The east face of the Maroon Bells from Pyramid Peak. If the traverse from North Maroon to Maroon Peak looks exposed, it is!

ascent came three days after Hagerman and Harold Clark reached
the summit of North Maroon Peak via a difficult route angling
up the north face.

Following Hagerman and Clark's pioneering climbs, the Maroon Bells became a favorite for Colorado Mountain Club parties.
A particular highlight came during the club's 1928 Annual Outing,
when an overnight excursion over Buckskin Pass from a Snowmass Lake base camp was made to climb the two peaks. One
marvels that more injuries did not occur in these early years,
given the large numbers usually in the climbing party. The Colorado Mountain Club Labor Day Outing of 1940 put 73 people
into base camp; 40 people were in the climbing party to attempt
to ascend the Bells. On this climb, two injuries did occur when
two climbers strayed from the main group and were struck by
falling rocks.

More often than not, the recent history of the Bells has been
one of tragedy — tragedy brought about not so much by inexperi-
ence, as by a lack of respect for the unforgiving nature of the
peaks. Rarely do they give a second chance. A September 1952
tragedy took the life of Gordon Schindel and severely injured
his climbing companion, Larry Hackstaff. Both experienced climbers, they began a traverse from North Maroon to Maroon Peak
late in the afternoon and lost control while descending the
treacherous, snow-filled couloir running northeast off the first
main sub-peak south of Maroon Peak. Only one climber carried
an ice axe.

The year of "The Deadly Bells" was 1965. In July, an Outward
Bound instructor was knocked to his death off a ledge by falling
rock. Several weeks later, three scientists from the University of
California's Los Alamos Scientific Laboratory in Los Alamos, New
Mexico, all experienced climbers (one was Herbert E. Ungnade,
author of *Guide to the New Mexico Mountains*), fell to their
deaths while roped together on a snowfield west of Maroon Peak.
A fourth member survived the 1,000-foot fall only because he
wore a hardhat.

During the following April, two Western State College students were killed in a fall while descending the standard northeast
couloir route. A third member survived the fall. Incredibly, the
climb to the summit had taken 14½ hours; then, when cold
discouraged a high-altitude bivouac, they began a moonlit des-

cent to their deaths. While each tragedy had multiple causes, the elements of ice axe, hardhat, and time schedule should be evident.

In the early 1970s, attention in the Elks focused on German-born skier and mountaineer Fritz Stammberger. He climbed North Maroon solo in February 1971 and Maroon Peak with Mike Pokress in December 1971, but the act that had Aspen buzzing was his daring ski descent of the North Bell. On June 24, 1971, after carefully calculating a line of snow-filled ledges and gullies, Stammberger climbed the route first and then made a 48-minute descent down the north face.

T H E   R O U T E S

From Aspen, drive west on Colorado 82 to just across Castle Creek, one mile, then south nine and one-half miles to Maroon Lake Campground (9,600 feet). From the campground, hike southwest along a well-beaten path for one and one-half miles to Crater Lake, then west for just over a half mile on the trail up Minnehaha Gulch to Buckskin Pass. Where the trail begins to level and a number of campsites dot the south side of the trail, descend south one hundred feet to the creek and climb south up a prominent gully topped by what in summer looks like a round, rocky island surrounded by a sea of green grass.

Cross the huge rock glacier beneath the north face of the North Bell southeast to a cairn-marked (cairn is difficult to see) trail along the first prominent ledge below the face. Follow the ledge across the strata of the northeast face to a rocky couloir. While not always visible, orange dots mark the route from here. Make a mental note of the exit point for the ledge on return and climb west up the couloir, through a crack at its head, and then left (southwest) to a ridge separating it from another couloir. From the ridge separating the two couloirs, keep to the south (left) of the main ridge to the top of the second couloir and then cross the ridge onto the upper part of the north face at 13,800 feet. A 20-foot crack with an orange dot and a large boulder at its head mark the route onto a short catwalk ridge and then up the remaining ridge to the summit. On a clear, dry day, the route is obvious, but the complexity of the mountain can spell disaster in inclement weather. For the North Bell only, return the same way.

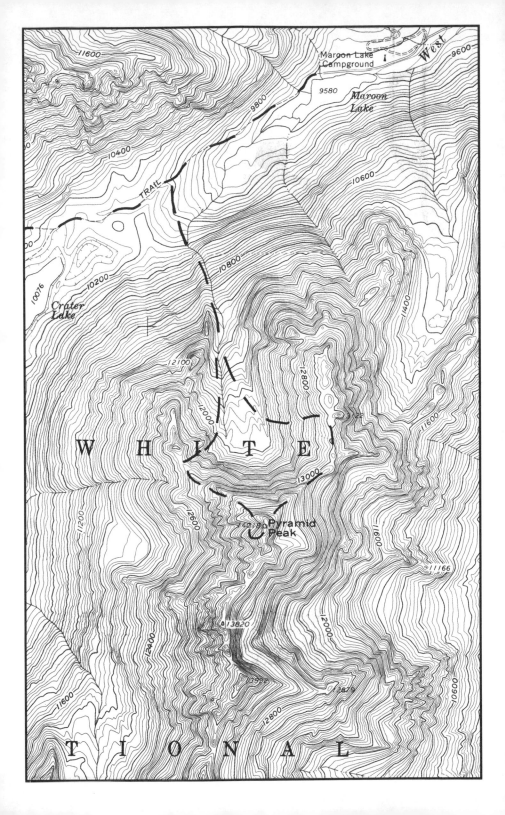

For the traverse, descend south from the North Bell down a loose and steep section and then along the ridge, staying on top or just to the west to the lowest saddle. At the low point, traverse slightly to the east, and then take a clear shot for the summit of Maroon Peak. No cairns or paint dots mark the traverse. The traverse takes at least one and one-half hours and should be attempted only if time and weather permit the long haul off Maroon Peak. Many parties desire the protection of a rope. Jim Gehres notes that the traverse from south to north is easier because one climbs up rather than down the most exposed portion and then has a shorter descent off North Maroon, although care must be taken in locating the correct descent route.

From Maroon Peak, descend via the south ridge, remaining on top of the ridge amid possibly the worst rock of the trip. Loose and rotten! Circle the deep cut of the couloir, which descends east from the 13,753-foot sub-peak, on the west and drop several hundred feet off the ridge to the west for about a half-mile. Regain the ridge and follow it south for a half-mile to a ridge just south of a broad but crumbling couloir leading east to West Maroon Creek, two miles above (south of) Crater Lake. A descent via the 13,753-foot sub-peak couloir should be made only by experienced parties equipped with ice axes. For the South Bell alone, follow the descent route.

Maroon Lake to North Bell summit: 4 miles; 4,400 feet.

Maroon Lake and Maroon Bells traverse (roundtrip): 9 miles; 4,800 feet.

A number of technical routes, including west face approaches from Snowmass Creek and the dike route on the North Bell's north ridge, exist. All should be treated with extreme care.

▲

Capitol Peak

14,130 feet (30th highest)

Like the giant throne — the capitol, indeed, of some noble monarch — Capitol thrusts its summit skyward amid an intricacy of long, narrow ridges. It is a mountain easily recognized from a distance and one on which the summit is usually in view to climbers attacking its heights. The mountain was named by the Hayden Survey for its resemblance to the U.S. Capitol Building, but no attempt was made to climb it because, in Henry Gannett's words, its "prism-shaped top and precipitous sides forbid access."

Apparently, Gannett's assessment of the peak held true until the days of Percy Hagerman and Harold Clark's (see Pyramid) forays into the Elks. Hagerman and Clark climbed Capitol on August 22, 1909, and Hagerman later reported that "as far as we can learn no other party has ever been on Capitol Peak. There was no evidence on the summit of any previous ascent and the peak was reputed to be unclimbed and unclimbable by ranchmen living in its neighborhood." Their route was via the northeast ridge which Hagerman described as doubtless the easiest, despite the fact that they negotiated the knife-edge on hands and knees — a procedure familiar to numerous later climbers of the peak.

Capitol is without a doubt one of the most difficult of the Fourteeners to climb and one which offers nontechnical climbers only one approach — the knife-edge ridge. Yet, there are those who would dispute a 1946 *Rocky Mountain News* headline hailing it Colorado's *most* difficult peak. Certainly the question is more academic than practical when one considers such variables as routes, rock stability, and weather. What is true is that Capitol's firmer rock (when compared to the Bells) has led to a number of fine technical climbs.

Capitol's dramatic 1,800-foot north face has lured a number of rock climbers, beginning with the 1937 ascent by Carl Blaurock, Elwyn Arps, and Harold Popham. Although subsequent climbs were made, for years the standing winter debate of Aspen barrooms centered around who would be the first to scale

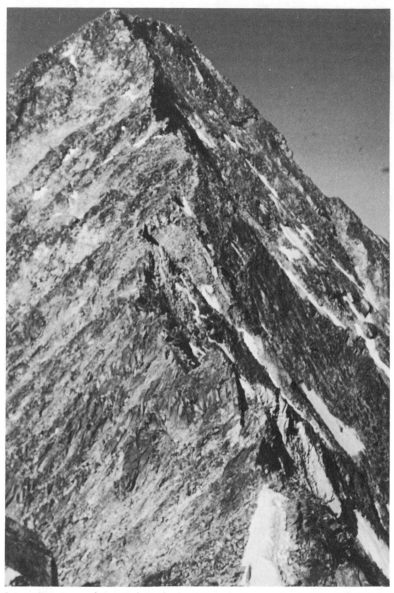

Summit prism of Capitol Peak, looking southwest from K2. The knife-edged ridge runs directly toward this camera.

Capitol's north face in winter and the god-like qualities such a person would have to possess. The gods turned out to be Aspen's own Fritz Stammberger (see Maroon Peak) and Gordon Whitmer, who reached the summit after 11 hours of face climbing on March 10, 1972. The north-face ascent came only six years after the first winter ascent of Capitol via the knife-edge in January of 1966.

T H E   R O U T E S

Snowmass Creek

From the Snowmass Lake trailhead (see Snowmass), hike west and then south on the Snowmass Lake Trail for one mile to just past a series of beaver ponds and a fenced gate, where the trail to Snowmass Lake continues up the valley along the east side of Snowmass Creek. Ford Snowmass Creek — a wet and very cold experience, which may even require a belay at peak runoff — and then hike west through an old homestead (a natural spot for some Colorado Thoreau) on a trail which climbs two miles up West Snowmass Creek before emerging into a delightful meadow at 9,800 feet. Here, the main trail continues west up Haystack Mountain and eventually loops back into Hunter Creek. Continue south across the meadow, which becomes a thinly disguised bog in the early summer. The best bet is to stay to the west of the low point and then angle back to the east of the main stream above it. This is the route that a trail, heavily veiled in most places, takes. It deposits you two miles up the valley at timberline at a series of small lakes and a suitable camp.

From camp, climb west up the broad slope into the basin just east of the rugged K-2-Daly ridge. For those not wishing to attack the ridge at its low point, angle southwest up the basin to K-2's summit (13,664 feet). Here the fun begins! Take care not to lunge immediately for the knife-edge! K-2 drops off sharply into Pierre Lakes Basin! Instead, contour down K-2's north side to the ridge and proceed to do one of Colorado's most noted and talked about routes — Capitol's knife-edge. While there are those daredevils who insist on tightrope walking the entire route, on a clear day the firm rock of the ridge (a welcome though uncommon occurrence in the Elks) requires little more than a steady pair of hands and a little gusto. As always, however, poor weather can turn it into a nightmare. Once across the knife-edge,

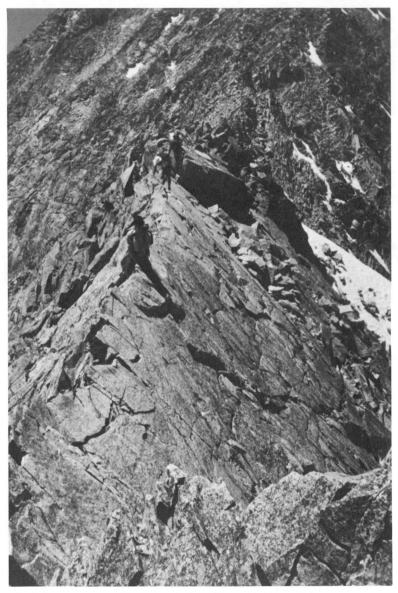

Climbers returning across Capitol Peak's Knife Edge Ridge.

Capitol's rock becomes loose and dangerous for the remainder of the route, which crosses the east face and then climbs west to the summit. Climbing to the northeast ridge when practical avoids the section of extremely loose rock southeast of the summit.

Snowmass trailhead to Summit: 7 miles; 5,800 feet.

Capitol Lake

This is the traditional approach to Capitol. From the Snowmass Post Office on Colorado 82, take the paved road south up Snowmass Creek for two miles, then the right-hand (west) fork six miles to the Capitol Creek guard station and one and one-half miles farther to the end of the passable road. The final one and one-half miles is extremely rough and can become very slippery when wet. A trail leads generally south from the meadow trailhead at 9,400 feet for six miles to Capitol Lake at 11,600 feet. From the lake, it is a steep half-mile scramble east to the Capitol-Daly saddle. From the saddle, K-2 and the knife-edge route described above is accessible via a tough, bouldering ridge directly south or by dropping over the saddle to the Snowmass Creek route.

Capitol Lake trailhead to Summit: 7½ miles; 4,700 feet; plus about 400 feet of elevation loss on the trail to the lake near the trailhead.

▲

Snowmass Mountain
14,092 feet (32nd highest)

The great snowfield which lies on the eastern flank of Snow-mass Mountain has long made it one of the most prominent summits seen from peaks well to the east. The striking beauty of the peak is furthered by its graceful, upward-sweeping ridges which encircle the better portion of the snowfield. Appropriately, this great peak is also a wilderness peak, and the eight and one-half mile trip into base camp at Snowmass Lake is the longest required into any Fourteener in the state and also affords one of the most scenic backpacking trips.

Because of its prominent but isolated location, Snowmass was sighted and used as a landmark long before it was climbed. The first recorded sighting of the peak was from Grays Peak in August 1869 by William Brewer, who noted "a great Snow Peak" on the western horizon just to the left of the Mount of the Holy Cross. Oddly enough, no formal name was given to this promi-nent summit until the Hayden Survey of 1873, but as miners penetrated the Elk Range, the two summits of Snowmass were known to them as "The Twins."

In 1873, a Hayden Survey team led by James Gardner entered the unknown valleys near Snowmass Mountain from the south, with a climb of the peak as one of their primary objectives. While their ascent route was from the south and not via the snowfield on the east, they were nonetheless very aware of the great expanse of snow, and they dubbed the mountain "Snowmass." Henry Gannett, however, overstated the nature of the snowfield when he reported that it had an area of five square miles and was probably the closest thing to a true glacier in the Rocky Moun-tains. In reality, the snowfield has an area of perhaps only one square mile, and large, true glaciers were later found in Wyom-ing's Wind River Range. Nevertheless, Snowmass was an accurate and descriptive name for the peak. The name persisted, despite some discussion among members of the survey to name it "Whitehouse" as a complement to nearby Capitol Peak.

Snowmass Mountain in the spring. This view looks west from Snowmass Lake across the snow-filled basin for which the peak is famous.

The first recorded ascent of Snowmass on August 7, 1873, was well documented and reported by members of the climbing team. William Byers climbed and carried the original account in his *Rocky Mountain News* later in the month. In the article, he quoted James Gardner as remarking that Snowmass was "the most difficult and dangerous climb he ever made," an understandable assessment considering that he carried a 40-pound transit while rock scrambling to the summit! Another account was later written by English author W. H. Rideing, guest of the survey, who commented that some of the party amused themselves by toppling over large boulders which went crashing down the slope, a practice definitely not recommended!

Before their work was completed on the peak, three separate ascents of Snowmass were made by the survey team. Snowmass provided an excellent vantage point into the heart of the Elks, and would have been a prime location for photographic work by William Henry Jackson, but the day he climbed, inclement weather set in, spoiling potentially high quality photographs. Since Snowmass was one of only two Elk Range Fourteeners climbed by the Hayden Survey, triangulation work from its summit was extensive, but they calculated Snowmass's height at only 13,970 feet, a figure not corrected until the twentieth century.

There was little mining activity in the immediate vicinity of Snowmass Mountain, but some silver mines operated in the 1880s and '90s in Lead King Basin, southwest of the peak and above the town of Crystal. Miners may have climbed Snowmass Mountain but probably not before the Hayden team in 1873. After the silver crash in 1893, the mines in Lead King Basin faded, and Snowmass Mountain returned to being one of the most isolated and least climbed Fourteeners in the state; that is, until the tremendous backpacking boom of the 1960s.

While James Gardner found Snowmass to be a tough climb, it is not difficult by the normal route when not carrying a 40-pound transit, but neighboring 13,841-foot Hagerman Peak, which thrusts 2,800 dramatic feet above Snowmass Lake, has seen some classic technical climbs. Technical routes on Snowmass have usually been traverses from either Hagerman or Capitol. Harold Clark made the first traverse of the difficult ridge between Snowmass and Hagerman in 1919. The first attemp at traversing the jagged, four-mile-long ridge connecting Snowmass and Capitol was made in 1951 by Bob Allen and Karl Gustafson, but they were turned back by lightning when almost to the summit of Snowmass. The traverse was finally successfully completed by Bill Forrest and Glen Denny in 1966.

T H E   R O U T E S

Snowmass Lake

The backpack into Snowmass Lake is one of the most popular trips in the Elk Range for backpacker, fisherman, photographer, and climber alike. As a result, the area is very heavily used in the summer; take extra care to leave as little trace as possible. Use restrictions and a permit system may soon be implemented.

The community (post office) of Snowmass is on Colorado 82, about 28 miles from Glenwood Springs and 14 miles from Aspen. Drive south from the post office up Snowmass Creek for about twelve and one-half miles to the Snowmass Creek trailhead at the road's terminus at 8,400 feet. The old Snowmass campground has been closed for some years and other camping

arrangements must be made. Another road from Aspen reaches the trailhead and is shorter, but it has a steep downgrade section. For this approach, take the road to Snowmass Village, six miles west of Aspen on Colorado 82, for six miles and then keep right on an unpaved road. Take this about two and a half miles to a junction, and take a left one-half mile to the trailhead parking lot.

Backpack up the excellent Snowmass Lake Trail past the Snowmass Falls Ranch and continue on the east side of the creek to about mile 6, where a series of large beaver ponds have dammed up the stream. At this point, there may be some trail confusion, for a trail also appears traversing uphill on the opposite (west) side of the stream. However, it is best to remain on the trail on the east side of the stream along the rocky talus slope and pass through the willows around the left of the ponds until the trail comes to a large log jam which it crosses to the west side of the stream. Shortly thereafter, the trail switchbacks up the hillside, and you gain 800 feet in the final one and one-half miles to Snowmass Lake, at almost 11,000 feet.

The conspicuous peak rising directly southwest of the lake is Hagerman Peak, and Snowmass Mountain is the hump directly above the rolling expanse of the snowfield basin to the right of Hagerman. The actual summit is the central highpoint of this hump. Pick your way around the left (southeast) shore of the lake and up the steep talus slope at the southwest end of the lake and into the snowfield basin. Until late summer, a great amount of snow may lie in this basin, and although the snow itself is freezing, it reflects a high percentage of the sun's rays, and the basin can be unbearably hot; skin and eye protection is vital.

Cross the basin west for about one mile until below the rocky southeast ridge of Snowmass. If steep snow lies along the east side of the southeast ridge, an ice axe is handy, and spring climbers will do well to be extremely wary of avalanche danger when gaining the ridge. The rounded end portion of the ridge to the left of the summit appears to be the easiest section to gain, but involves considerably more rock scrambling once on top than routes which gain the ridge more to the northwest. Scramble up the east slope of the ridge well north of the end point, or up the couloir, which leads to the ridge just before it suddenly steepens to the final summit block. Either way, you will end up within a half-mile of the summit on the broken ridge. The ridge may look tough, but the rock is generally sound and offers excellent handholds when they are needed. Snowmass is a good introduction to bouldering without the necessity of a rope. Stay on top of the ridge or just to the left (west) of it for the remaining distance to the summit.

Snowmass Lake to Summit: 2½ miles; 3,100 feet.

Parking lot to Snowmass Lake: 8½ miles; 2,600 feet.

It is also possible to climb Snowmass via a south southwest ridge from Geneva Lake above Lead King Basin, as the Hayden Survey men did, but as they reported, this route involves some loose rock. What they did *not* report is that it also involves a section of tough jeep road between Marble and the ghost town of Crystal before the trailhead to the lake is reached.

▲

Sentinels of a Spanish Legacy: The Sangre de Cristo Range

Unique in many respects, the Sangre de Cristo Range defies comparison with other ranges in Colorado. While other Colorado ranges have histories intimately tied with the Anglo mining rushes of the 1800s, the Sangre de Cristo Range is tied more closely with the history and culture of the Southwest; indeed, its snow-capped peaks may have been known to the Spanish as early as 1600. Geographically, the Sangre de Cristo is long and narrow, rising to a sharp crest with a minimum of foothills, quite unlike the more massive, rolling character of most of the other ranges in the state. Finally, even the geology of the Sangre de Cristo range does not fit the mold of most of the state's ranges. Many of its geologic complexities are still being unraveled.

The southermost range in the Rocky Mountain chain, the Sangre de Cristo Range runs for about 200 miles from south of Salida well into New Mexico, terminating in the vicinity of Santa Fe. Approximately 115 miles of the range lies in Colorado, and it averages only 10 to 20 miles in width. To the west, the Sangre de Cristos are flanked by the expansive San Luis Valley, which is drained by the Rio Grande River; to the east, the Wet Mountain Valley and Huerfano Park border a substantial portion of the range.

The crest of the Sangre de Cristos lies almost 7,000 feet above the San Luis and Wet Mountain valleys, making it one of Colorado's steepest ranges overall. As a result, though the range is highly visible, few roads penetrate it and even fewer cross it.

The geology of the Sangre de Cristos has not been studied thoroughly, but the northern part of the range is basically a fault block structure. A fault block range differs from an anticlinal range in that it is lifted as a block with complete breaking of overlying rock layers along at least one side, rather than arching and folding. These overlying Paleozoic layers have been eroded from the crest of the range north of Hayden Pass, but are present on the very crest of the range to the south. The most notable of these sedimentary layers for the mountaineer is the Crestone Conglomerate, whose plentiful nubs and projections make for a rock climber's delight on Crestone Needle.

About 20,000 years ago, long after the major glaciers had disappeared, Colorado became semi-arid in climate. This warming and drying had the greatest effect on vegetation, and once lush valley floors became only sparsely vegetated. As a result, winds blowing across the wide valley floor of the San Luis Valley picked up a tremendous amount of topsoil and sand. In the San Luis Valley, winds have a tendency to funnel toward Mosca and Music passes, and, as they rise, they are unable to carry all the sand over the mountains, and so deposit it along the western foothills of the Sangre de Cristos. In 20,000 years, these deposits of sand have accumulated to depths of up to 700 feet and formed one of the most interesting and distinctive features of the Sangre de Cristos, the Great Sand Dunes.

Following the founding of Santa Fe in 1609, Spanish missionaries and explorers gradually penetrated the country to the north. As they went, they gave names to prominent geographic features. The most common explanation for designating the range "Sangre de Cristo," or "Blood of Christ," is that an unknown explorer or missionary viewed the reflection of a deep red sunset upon its peaks, and in a moment of inspiration, gave the range the religious name. It is not known exactly how early the Spaniards used this name, but Anglo references to the name appeared in the early 1800s.

In 1820, Mexico declared its independence from Spain, and the new government granted large parcels of land along its northern frontier to encourage settlement. Six of these grants were wholly or partially in what is now Colorado, and two of these encompassed sizeable portions of the Culebra Range. The Vigil and St. Vrain Grant occupied the eastern slope of the Culebra Range, the southern one-half of the Blanca massif, and a tremendous amount of land to the east. The Sangre de Cristo Grant bordered the Culebra Range on the west and included much of the southeastern San Luis Valley. Both of these grants were given in 1843, but attempts at settlements two years later were thwarted by Indian raids. In 1849, permanent settlement began in the San

Luis Valley; in 1851, the community of San Luis, Colorado's oldest town, was founded.

Most of the recent history in and around the Sangre de Cristos has revolved around agriculture and real estate development. In 1867, the Sangre de Cristo Grant was bought and divided into the Costilla and Trinchera estates, two of Colorado's first major real estate developments; the trend has continued ever since. Large land sales in the area have made access difficult into parts of the range and have also allowed for the only sole ownership of a Fourteener in the United States, Culebra Peak.

Crestone Peak
14,294 feet (7th highest)

Crestone Needle
14,197 feet (20th highest)

Kit Carson Peak
14,165 feet (23rd highest)

Humboldt Peak
14,064 feet (37th highest)

Search Colorado for the sheer and abrupt grandeur of Wyoming's Tetons and one name immediately comes to mind — the Crestones. Rugged, isolated, and unforgiving, Crestone Peak and Crestone Needle dominate an area of the central Sangre de Cristo which until 1967 did not even have an adequate topographic map. A certain veil of mystery and mystique surrounding the peaks dates from the earliest Spanish forays into the San Luis Valley. De Anza's 1779 ride around the Sangre de Cristos (see Part I) is well documented, but for every factual account, a dozen or more legends of wandering adventurers, lost mines, and buried treasure have come down through the years with just enough historical fact to give them credence.

Many of the legends center on the large and complex underground labyrinth of Marble Cave in Marble Mountain just southeast of the Crestones. Tales of Spaniards using Indian slaves to mine gold and silver and of entrances to the cave on both sides of the range have sent spelunkers probing its depths.

While "who did what where" will probably remain veiled in mystery, some Spanish adventurers and prospectors did scour

Crestone Peak from the north, high on Kit Carson Peak. The summit to the right (west) is the true summit, while the cliffs at the prominent couloir's base graphically demonstrate the need to exit before the couloir bends west. *R. Omar Richardson.*

the valleys of the Sangre de Cristo. The word "Crestone" itself is of Spanish derivation, meaning "the top of a cock's comb," "the crest of a helmet," or in miners' lexicon, "an outcropping of ore."

If the Spanish presence in the Sangre de Cristo is somewhat bewildering, equally so are Anglo attempts over the next century to name and map the peaks. Mountain men noticed the similarity between these peaks and Wyoming's Tetons and gave the name "Trois Tetons" to the Crestones and one of their neighbors, either Kit Carson Peak to the northwest or Broken Hand Peak to the south, depending on which account you prefer. The name "Trois Tetons" was duly recorded by Captain John Gunnison in his journal as he passed south of the peaks in 1853, seeking a trans-continental railroad route. Here, however, the story becomes a labyrinth of confusion. Until well into the 1900s, a wide variety of surveys placed Crestone Peak and Kit Carson in just about every location imaginable, interchanged the names, and even gave them just about every name imaginable! One 1882 map

Crestone Needle from Humboldt Peak: the non-technical route gains the saddle at left and then climbs to the summit via the second rib west of the skyline. Ellingwood Arete descends straight down from the summit. *R. Omar Richardson.*

did nothing to ease the Crestone-Trois Teton confusion by adding the names "Mount Celeste" and "Mount Julia" to the group. Even today, some old-timers in the town of Crestone on the San Luis Valley side insist on calling Kit Carson "Crestone Peak." Thus, tales of naming the peaks are almost as boundless as tales of buried Spanish treasure.

One bright light does shine through the veil to illuminate the naming and first ascent of Humboldt Peak. In sharp contrast to the rugged Crestones, Humboldt sprawls like a giant ant hill east into the Wet Mountain Valley from the high plateau separating Crestone Peak and Kit Carson. In the spring of 1870, Carl Wulsten, a Prussian immigrant and one-time Civil War general, led a band of German settlers into the Wet Mountain Valley in an attempt to establish the first cooperative community in Colorado. The group built homes, plowed fields, and planted crops to the southwest of present-day Westcliffe, naming their hoped-for utopia "Colfax," after the then Vice-President of the United States.

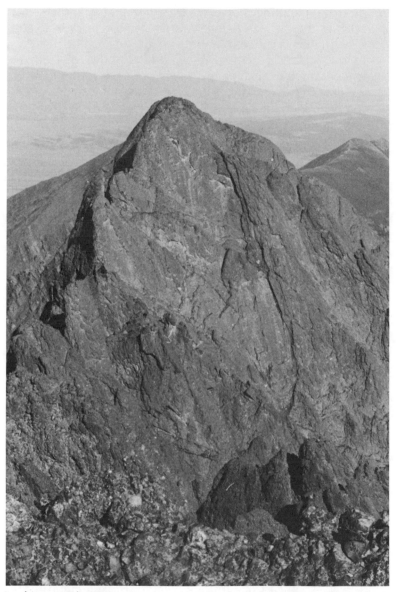

Looking southeast to Crestone Needle from the summit of Crestone Peak. As is obvious from the photo, the traverse is nothing to mess with in bad weather. *Craig F. Koontz.*

The promises of spring, however, were unfulfilled, and a series of problems, not the least being Wulsten's tactless leadership and a devastating fire, scattered the settlement.

In subsequent years, however, a large influx of German settlers continued to such valley towns as Ula, Rosita, Querida, Silver Cliff, and Westcliffe. Although primarily farmers, these newcomers mined the eastern slopes of the Sangre de Cristo. In 1874, Leonard Frederick located the Humboldt mine near the slopes of what became known as Humboldt Peak. The name honored Alexander von Humboldt, an eminent German geographer, explorer, and mountaineer, who gained particular fame in mountaineering circles with an unsuccessful 1802 assault on Ecuador's Mount Chimborazo, then thought by some to be the highest peak in the world. As part of the Land Office Surveys of 1883, the peak was climbed, probably by surveyor T. P. Momson, and clearly recorded as Humboldt Peak. No serious attempt was made to penetrate the mountain walls to the west.

By 1916, the names of "Crestone Peak," "Crestone Needle," and "Kit Carson Peak" were reasonably well established on the peaks we know today, and, perhaps most significantly, were the only fourteen-thousand-foot peaks in Colorado that were unclimbed. In the summer of 1916, Albert R. Ellingwood, the grand master of early Colorado climbing (see La Plata Peak), and seven others made camp in the drainage of Willow Creek northwest of the peaks in high spirits, in Ellingwood's words, "fed by tales of peaks unclimbed and peaks unclimbable." The party ascended the northwest ridge of Kit Carson, scrambled over the northwest sub-peak (14,080 feet), and made the first documented ascent of Kit Carson.

Kit Carson, of course, was named for the famous scout who, in the mid-1860s, commanded the garrison at Fort Garland at the foot of Blanca Peak. Here too, local legend and lore run deep with some asserting that the great scout lived in a cabin near the peak's base for several years. A rip-roaring contemporary of old Kit's was Indian agent Thomas FitzPatrick, whose Indian name, "Broken Hand," is remembered in 13,573-foot Broken Hand Peak, southeast of Crestone Needle. Broken Hand is the first prominent landmark that climbers see as they navigate the South Colony road, and more than one group has mistaken it for Crestone Peak — a mistake which is soon apparent when the

Kit Carson Peak, looking north from Crestone Peak, showing the recently named Challenger Point in the distance. *Craig F. Koontz*.

Needle looms into view.

With one down and two to go, "the more energetic of the party," Ellingwood, Eleanor Davis, Frances "Bee" Rogers, and Joe Deutchbein, moved their camp south to the Spanish Creek drainage to test, in Ellingwood's words, "the unclimbability of the Crestones." On July 24, 1916, the quartet got an exceptionally late (8:10 A.M.) start and proceeded up Crestone's north arete and into the north couloir, reaching the summit of the main peak at 12:40. After constructing a cairn on each of the twin summits (Ellingwood incorrectly guessed the eastern point was higher), the party gingerly began the traverse to the Needle. Ellingwood found, as have later climbers, that "progress on the ridge was most encouraging, for the gendarmes that stood up like Cleopatra's Needle on the east were of a gentler aspect on the other side and lent themselves to prudential circumvention." Half-way across, Deutchbein, who was troubled with a bad knee, and Miss Rogers returned to the Spanish Creek camp, but Ellingwood and Miss Davis continued the traverse, finishing on the conglomerate-studded northwest wall of the Needle. Here,

The plaque placed atop Challenger Point on Kit Carson Peak, looking south to the Sand Dunes and Blanca massif. *Alan Silverstein*.

Ellingwood and Davis built a third cairn and claimed the last unclimbed Fourteener in the state. As twilight approached, the pair hurried down the southeast ridge, glimpsed the prominent eastern arete, skirted the South Colony Lakes, and returned to their campsite via the Crestone-Humboldt saddle, arriving beleagueredly at 11:15 P.M.

Once conquered, the peaks continued to lure only a handful of climbers during the next decade. Eleanor Davis and Albert Ellingwood with Stephen H. Hart and Marion Warner returned in August of 1925 to pioneer the classic eastern arete of Crestone Needle, now known as "Ellingwood Arete." The 1925 Annual Outing of the Colorado Mountain Club made a traverse of Crestone Needle to the Peak, only its fifth recorded ascent. As late as September of 1929, *Trail and Timberline* reported only the fifth ascent of Kit Carson.

With climbing interest increasing, the peaks withstood one more attempt to confuse their names. In 1923, the Colorado Mountain Club officially added the name "Crestone Needle" to its list of high points. A year later, club member Roger Toll suggested changing Crestone Needle to "Mallory Peak" and North Maroon Peak to "Mount Irvine." Mallory and Irvine's names were on the lips of the climbing world for their mysterious disappearance the preceding spring while high in the mists of Mount Everest. Nothing was done, however, and the matter quickly dropped; yet, Crestone Needle was again suggested for a name change in 1976 when members of the Colorado Centennial-Bicentennial Commission were searching for a peak to christen "Centennial Peak." A visit by one Commission member to the town of Crestone revealed that old-timers might call Kit Carson "Crestone" and vice versa, but they did not want any part of "Centennial Peak." The name was finally bestowed on Banded Mountain, an inconspicuous sub-peak of Hesperus Peak in the La Platas.

The 1,000-foot northeast wall of the Crestones has become a favorite for rock climbers with such climbing greats as Bob Ormes, Bill House, Dick Pownall, and Bill Forrest pioneering technical climbs. The face must rank with the north faces of Blanca and Capitol as one of Colorado's most challenging rock climbs. The challenges of winter ascents were met in the 1960s, culminating in a traverse of the Needle to the Peak on March

Humboldt Peak from the west looking across the pinnacles of the Crestone Needle to Peak ridge. *Craig F. Koontz.*

17, 1972, by a party of Pat McGrane, Charles Campbell, and John Rehmer, which ended with a forced bivouac at 13,300 feet on Crestone Peak.

The unforgiving nature of these peaks was dramatized in June 1979, when four young climbers plummetted to their deaths while making a roped descent on Kit Carson's north face. The three teenage boys and their young adult leader were members of an expedition from a Missouri-based troubled teen program. The four were roped and equipped with ice axes and were apparently descending the snowfields above upper Willow Lake after an attempt on the northwest ridge of Kit Carson when they got off route and fell to their deaths.

In recent years, the death toll on the Crestones has been every bit as grim as the "deadly Bells." John Holyoke, an experienced and veteran climber, died on Crestone Peak in 1981. The following year Matthew O'Connor and Dave Madsen died in separate accidents involving long falls on Crestone Needle. These mountains are unforgiving.

In 1987, the 14,081-foot northwest sub-peak of Kit Carson

was named Challenger Point, commemorating the crew members of the space shuttle Challenger who lost their lives on January 28, 1986. A bronze plaque was placed on the summit on July 19, 1987, by a party led by Alan Silverstein.

T H E   R O U T E S

South Colony Lakes

When the nominations are made for the paradise of Colorado, the Wet Mountain Valley rolling up the green flanks of the Sangre de Cristo Range to the summits of the Crestones must surely be among them. From Westcliffe, drive south on Colorado 69 for about four and one-half miles to Colfax Lane, then right (south) on Colfax Lane for five more miles until it comes to a "T" intersection and turns west, climbs through several fence lines, and becomes increasingly rocky. Most cars stop at the Forest boundary, although jeeps and an occasional Volkswagen have made it six miles more to the end of the trail beneath Broken Hand Peak.

From the end of the road, lower South Colony Lake is one-half mile north along a well-used trail. Large parties should use any number of campsites along the road, but smaller groups will find several ideal cmapsites near the lakes. This is definitely one of those spots that should be attempted, if at all possible, during the week. Weekends have seen minor traffic jams, to say the least.

From South Colony Lakes, Humboldt is the easily distinguishable ant-hill-type mountain one mile to the northeast. It is an easy climb from the lakes, providing that one puts up with combinations of talus and scree. Farther down (east) the valley from the lakes, the climb gets steeper and leads one into the very prominent avalanche chutes which frequently discharge their burden of white death in the early spring. Humboldt offers an unparalleled view of the Crestones and the routes on Crestone Peak and Kit Carson.

Lower South Colony Lake to Humboldt: 1½ miles; 2,400 feet.

Ah yes, the Crestones! What a contrast in rock stability within yards! The route up the Needle from the south is on solid rock with plenty of handholds. The route in the north-face couloir of Crestone Peak is crumbly and frequently icy and slick. The Nee-

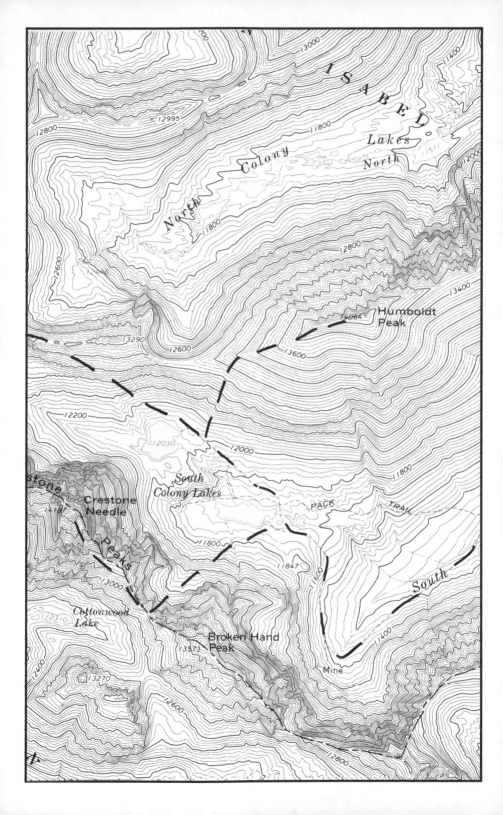

dle and Peak are frequently climbed together; the south to north (the Needle to Peak) traverse is the easier way. Individual climbs do best to follow the directions given for that peak in the traverse description. From the lakes, climb southwest to the low point of the Needle's southeast ridge, a route marked with cairns. Atop the ridge, a cairn-marked trail leads north into the second prominent rock gully. The first gully is steeper and airier, but it also ends up on the summit. The couloir is steep and a little airy, but the rock is superb, and handholds are plentiful, once the summer sun has emptied the place of ice and snow. The couloir climbs straight up to just southeast of the summit, and then it's northwest on the ridge several hundred feet to the top. For the Needle only, return the same way.

The traverse to the Peak is long, but not particularly difficult once one is down the first pitch northwest of the Needle's summit. A fixed rope or rappel will make the 100 feet from Needle summit to ridge more secure. The rock is conglomerate with ample handholds, but since one false step will deposit one a thousand feet down the east face, more timid and frequently wiser souls enjoy the use of a rope. The trick to the Needle-peak traverse is to drop down the southwest couloirs of the ridge just enough to avoid the spires on the ridge proper, but not so far that one loses precious elevation. The goal is the red couloir and saddle, very visible from most of the ridge, which runs within 200 feet of the Peak's summit. Climbing to the ridge before the red couloir will require skirting the 14,000-foot point east of the red saddle. Upon reaching the red saddle, climb left (west) to the summit.

From the summit of the Peak, return to the red saddle and descend the north couloir, a painful array of smooth slab rock sprinkled with sand, ice, and loose rock. As the couloir swings increasingly northwest, exit to the north at the first opportunity. The point is about 1,000 feet in elevation below the saddle and a few hundred feet above the sharp cliffs at the couloir's foot. (This makes a spectacular photograph from Kit Carson.) The exit drops one into a large plateau, the Bears Playground, between Kit Carson and the Peak. From here, the route swings east, skirts the Peak's northeast ridge, offers a fantastic silhouette of the Needle with Ellingwood Arete on the left-hand skyline, and drops down a scree-filled couloir to the upper lake.

For Kit Carson, mount the Bears Playground via any of the

couloirs leading northwest from the upper lake. Contour across the north side of the plateau, angling for the highest visible point, which is the east false summit of Kit Carson (not the 13,800 point directly north of the plateau). With steep sides to the north and south, it is just as easy to climb over the false summit as to traverse. Then descend on the west southwest side of the sub-peak via a series of chutes and cracks into the bottom of a rather dramatic cut. The climb is steep, but the route obvious and the rock firm. Scramble across the cut and up the final 500 feet to Kit Carson's summit, amid generally loose talus and scree.

   Lower South Colony Lake to Crestone Needle: 1 mile; 2,500 feet.

   Lower South Colony Lake to Crestone Peak: 2½ miles; 2,600 feet.

   Lower South Colony Lake to Needle-Peak traverse, roundtrip: 4 miles; 3,000 feet, but hard.

   Lower South Colony Lake to Kit Carson: 2½ miles; 2,850 feet, plus 350 feet on return over sub-peak.

   A number of fine routes also exist on Kit Carson from the Willow Creek and Spanish Creek drainages of the San Luis Valley. Similar approaches for the Peak and Needle still involve the described upper routes, although from Cottonwood Creek an easier route ascends the gully leading to the red couloir on the Peak.

▲

Blanca Peak

14,345 feet (4th highest)

Ellingwood Peak

14,042 feet (43rd highest)

Little Bear Peak

14,037 feet (44th highest)

The Sierra Blanca abounds in those things which make great mountains great — a dominating position overlooking the vastness of the San Luis Valley, steep peaks whose great rock faces beckon the mountaineer, and a rich and colorful history. The king peak of the Sierra Blanca is Blanca Peak, and it is encircled with a number of lesser summits, creating such a striking hierarchy of form that Franklin Rhoda noted in 1875 that "such a beautiful subordination of parts we had not seen before anywhere among the mountains of Colorado." Over one hundred years later, few mountaineers who stand upon Blanca's summit would disagree with Rhoda's assessment of the magnificent Sierra Blanca.

A landmark since the prehistoric settlers of the San Luis Valley, the Sierra Blanca has watched the march of the Ute, Spanish, and Anglo cultures across the valleys around its base. Spanish influence is seen in the name "Sierra Blanca," meaning simply "White Mountain," probably applied because snow is visible high on the massif throughout the year. The name appears as early as E. G. Beckwith's report of the Gunnison expedition of 1853, but it may have been used much earlier by the Spanish. Blanca became the name of the highest summit of the Sierra at an early date, but "Little Bear" and "Ellingwood" were not given as names until much later.

The first recorded ascent of Blanca Peak was on August 14,

The north face of Blanca Peak, with Ellingwood Peak to the right, from the upper Huerfano Valley. *Colorado Historical Society.*

1874, by Gilbert Thompson and Frank Carpenter of the Wheeler Survey; yet, much to their surprise, they found a man-made stone breastwork on the summit. Undoubtedly, the Utes had climbed the peak and used it as a lookout, or perhaps it was the work of some adventuresome Spaniard out to see what was up there. Blanca was one of the few Fourteeners on which the Wheeler Survey preceded the Hayden Survey; yet, characteristically, it is the Hayden Survey's record, thanks again to the recording detail of Franklin Rhoda, which is more complete. Rhoda climbed the peak with A. D. Wilson and Frederic Endlich on June 19, 1875. His account is rich in detail and is published in some length in Bueler's *Roof of the Rockies*. Rhoda made note of Old Baldy (Lindsey), and without naming it, Little Bear. Another Hayden party climbed Blanca the following year, and in the 1876 report, Wilson gave the peak an elevation of 14,413 feet, then thought to be the highest in the state.

After the surveys' ascents of Blanca, the possibility that the peak was the highest in the Rockies made it a natural goal for the venturesome mountaineer. In 1888, Charles Fay and J. R.

Edmands set out to ascend Blanca, but in the confusion of ridges and valleys, found themselves standing on the summit of West Peak instead. Between West Peak and Blanca itself lay a one and one-half mile narrow ridge which Rhoda had described as being "perfectly impassable to man." While Fay disputed Rhoda's opinion, he and Edmands decided that time did not permit attempting a traverse, and so they descended. While Fay and Edmands failed to reach Blanca on this climb, what they perhaps did not realize was that their climb of West Peak (now Little Bear) was certainly a first ascent. A difficult peak, Little Bear was seldom climbed until the mid-1900s. The name change was made in 1916, and John Jerome Hart states that the peak acquired the name of "Little Bear Creek" at its foot, but the 1965 Twin Peaks Quadrangle shows no sign of Little Bear Creek, only Little Bear Lake, suggesting that the name of the creek has been changed since 1916.

The spectacular ridges and great faces of the Sierra Blanca inevitably attracted some of the foremost rock climbers of the twentieth century. The greatest face in the Sierra is the one-mile-wide and 1,500-foot-high north face of Blanca and Ellingwood peaks. The first ascent of this face was by Robert Ormes and Harold Wilm in 1927. A more direct route up this face was pioneered by a Colorado College team in 1948, and other routes have become increasingly popular in recent years. Blanca's tough northeast ridge may have been first climbed by Enos Mills in an early 1900s winter ascent, but details in his *Spell of the Rockies* are extremely sketchy — so much so that it is not certain whether he climbed Blanca or some other peak in the vicinity. The first verified ascent of the northeast ridge was made by Carl Blaurock and Mary Cronin in 1937. Blanca's southeast face remained unclimbed until 1938, when Joe Merhar and others successfully scaled it.

While most of the attention has focused on Blanca, neighboring Little Bear has also seen some technical climbing. Little Bear's most imposing side, its 1,200-foot east face, has impressed many climbers, but as of 1988, it remained unconquered, perhaps the highest unclimbed face in Colorado. In 1931, Rhoda's "impassable" ridge between Little Bear and Blanca was first traversed by Joe Merhar and Dale Norton, who thereby conquered what may be the toughest connecting ridge between any two Fourteeners in the state. In the early days, Little Bear was climbed by its

Ellingwood Peak from the southwest, as seen from above Lake Como.

south ridge, probably the easiest route, but in 1943, Carl Blaurock, Roy Murchison, and Herb Hollister ascended Little Bear via Como Lake Basin and the west ridge, which in Hollister's words, "had plenty of everything wrong with it that any ridge could have." On September 1, 1956, tragedy struck on Little Bear when Banks Caywood fell to his death while descending the west side of the peak. It had become clear that Little Bear had no "easy" route, and the peak remains one of Colorado's most challenging Fourteeners.

One-half mile northwest of Blanca Peak is Ellingwood Peak, which has recently been recognized as a separate Fourteener. While the status of Ellingwood Peak was once disputed, the achievements of its namesake are not (see La Plata Peak). Since Ellingwood was neglected for so many years, no records of a first ascent are available, but it is probable that it was climbed before the twentieth century, since it is located so near Blanca Peak. In recent years, as mentioned, Ellingwood's northeast face has seen a number of technical climbs.

Some prospecting and mining was done in the Sierra Blanca through the 1930s, but none of the strikes were exceedingly rich. In 1899, free gold was discovered in Big Bear Canyon, in the vicinity of Bear Lake (now Lake Como). The original claim was the Commodore, and a small mining camp known as Commodore Camp was laid out in the canyon. The camp was never more than just that — a mining camp — and was short-lived as ownership disputes over the Commodore halted production before the area boomed. Even false rumors of a fantastic gold strike on the very summit of Blanca Peak in 1932 failed to bring eager prospectors to the area, and today only scattered remains in the basins below Blanca Peak remind the hiker and mountaineer of the prospectors' broken dreams.

In recounting the history of Blanca Peak, it would be an oversight to ignore the exploits of Donald E. Bennett, one-time Alamosa radio announcer. As is understandable, Bennett was quite fond of Blanca Peak, which is highly visible from Alamosa. Perhaps not quite so understandable are the lengths to which Bennett went to have Blanca publicized and calculated as the highest peak in Colorado, if not in all of the 48 United States. Bennett's promotions began in 1935 with an Easter Sunrise Service on the summit of the peak. Forty-three people trudged through

Little Bear Peak from the Lake Como Basin, with its west ridge running to the right. *R. Omar Richardson.*

waist-deep snow to sing "The Old Rugged Cross" and "Rock of Ages" on the summit. The following year, Bennett again organized a sunrise service for Easter, but as an added feature, Miss Helen Jacks and D. J. Edgar were to be married on the summit immediately following the service. As things turned out, only about one-half of the 30 who started the climb made the summit, and the couple were actually married in a cabin below timberline.

The semi-failure of the 1936 expedition did not stop Don Bennett, however. In 1939, Bennett began concentrated efforts to prove that Blanca was the highest point in Colorado. Convinced that modern calculations of the peak's height were too low, Bennett took it upon himself to aid in the measurement of the peak. In August of 1939, he attempted to erect a 50-foot pole on the summit of the peak which was equipped with a reflector at the top from which surveyors could make accurate measurements, and then subtract 50 feet to obtain the height of the peak. In his first attempt, Bennett failed to erect the entire pole on the summit because of the small space and high winds, but he nonetheless personally determined Blanca's elevation as 14,475 feet, by far the highest in Colorado.

When the whole affair was over, the U.S. Geological Survey failed to give Blanca any better than fourth place among Colorado's peaks, and Bennett abandoned his efforts once and for all. Interestingly enough, however, on the latest 7½' quadrangle of Blanca Peak, published in 1967, Blanca's elevation of 14,345 feet is printed as an unchecked elevation, the only such occurrence for any Colorado Fourteener mapped by the U.S. Geological Survey — just one more confusing detail in the saga of Blanca Peak's much-disputed elevation.

T H E   R O U T E S

Lake Como

Climbers who climb in the Sierra Blanca via the traditional routes usually have one of two basic photos among their records of the climb — either a "this-is-where-we-had-to-walk-from-in-the-middle-of-a-desert" photo or a "this-is-where-the-jeep-broke-down" photo. The Lake Como road is undoubtedly one of the roughest in the state. Its large boulders and sharp ledges have claimed the tires, U-joints, and transmissions of countless jeeps and would-be jeeps driven by even those worthy of a C. W. McCall recounting of their exploits. On Colorado 150, either three miles north of U.S. 160 or 14 miles south of Great Sand Dunes National Monument, turn east on a dirt road running almost directly northeast toward Blanca's summit. After two miles, the decision is usually made as to which type of picture the group will cherish, and the road switchbacks the remaining four and one-half miles up first Chokecherry and then Holbrook Canyons to Lake Como (11,740 feet). The lake has some private cabins around it, and camping is best done about a half-mile farther east up the valley amid some pines at timberline beneath the awesome hunk of Little Bear.

For Blanca and Ellingwood, continue northeast on a pack trail past Crater Lake for two miles and then angle east up the imposing but relatively easy west face of Blanca. For the traverse to Ellingwood, those who are willing to forego the scenic ridge route (the north side of the ridge drops sharply off the peaks'

north faces) find it easier to descend several hundred feet below the connecting saddle and then scramble up Ellingwood's southeast slopes. Both climbs are relatively easy while affording impressive views, particularly of Little Bear.

Lake Como to Blanca, Ellingwood traverse and return: 5 miles; 3,200 feet.

For Little Bear, from the camp area above Lake Como, climb directly south up the prominent couloir, tricky in late spring snow, to Little Bear's west ridge. Follow the ridge east until a sharp cut interrupts, dropping a steep couloir north into Como Basin. At the cut, leave the ridge and contour south, maintaining elevation and following a hit-and-miss assortment of cairns about a quarter of a mile to a narrow couloir which climbs directly to Little Bear's summit, 600 feet above. The couloir is extremely steep, filled with much loose rock, and is almost certain to have snow and ice in it, even late in the season. Use extreme caution. Once on top, the Little Bear-Blanca ridge is one of the classics, but should be attempted only by experienced parties when weather permits at least three hours on the tightrope.

Lake Como to Little Bear: 1 mile, 2,300 feet, but *tough* climbing!

Little Bear may also be climbed from Lake Como by a couloir and series of ledges leading to the Blanca ridge just north of the summit. Ellingwood and Blanca offer technical north face routes from Huerfano Canyon. Blanca's southeast face is a technical climb from the Winchell Lakes, but one must also contend with the uncertainty of private land access north of Fort Garland.

▲

Mount Lindsey

14,042 feet (42nd highest)

Rising only two miles east of well-known Blanca Peak, Mount Lindsey nonetheless retains an individuality in form and history quite apart from the Blanca Massif. While Blanca and its nearer satellites are angular and have some outstanding rock faces, Mount Lindsey is a comparatively smooth, massive cone, rising from the high mountain valleys in a single summit with few intervening foothills. In addition, while Blanca, Little Bear, and Ellingwood peaks have histories associated with many great climbers, Mount Lindsey was most familiar to primarily one man who held a deep love for the peak — that man was Malcolm Lindsey.

Mount Lindsey is highly visible from nearby valleys, and it was therefore natural that the peak would become a landmark for early settlers. Showing a remarkable lack of imagination, some observant pioneer noted the absence of trees on much of the peak and christened it "Old Baldy." When members of the Hayden Survey noted Old Baldy on their June 19, 1875, ascent of Blanca, they made no suggestions for changing the name, nor did they decide that an ascent of Old Baldy was necessary for their purposes. However, the peak was climbed by Wheeler men later in the year — the first official ascent. Missing a golden opportunity, the Wheeler Survey also failed to suggest a substitute name for Old Baldy, and the name remained for 78 more years.

In the years that followed, Old Baldy was one of the least climbed of all Colorado's Fourteeners, and it slumbered in relative obscurity until the arrival of Malcolm Lindsey. He was born in Pennsylvania in 1880 but grew up in Trinidad. There he became acquainted with the slopes of the peak that would one day bear his name, and he developed a genuine love for Old Baldy. In 1906, he was admitted to the Colorado Bar and subsequently practiced law in a number of the state's communities. He became legal counsel to the City of Denver in 1925 and then served as City Attorney from 1937 to 1947. Lindsey took an active part in community affairs, and he was a member of the Sons of The

Looking east to Mount Lindsey from the summit ridge of Ellingwood Peak. *Gary Koontz.*

American Revolution and a lay leader in the Episcopal Church for 48 years.

Malcolm Lindsey joined the Colorado Mountain Club in 1922 and became a vital force in that organization's junior activities; he led many groups of teenagers to the summit of Old Baldy. Lindsey served very ably on the State Board of Directors of the Colorado Mountain Club for many years, and was President from 1943-1946. It was with great sadness that members of the Colorado Mountain Club and the citizens of Denver noted his death on November 12, 1951.

In remembrance of Lindsey's years of service to the Colorado Mountain Club, members of that organization submitted a proposal to the United States Board of Geographic Names to change the name of Old Baldy to "Mount Malcolm Lindsey." On July 30, 1953, the name change was approved, and the designation of "Old Baldy" became the superbly appropriate "Mount Lindsey." Formal dedication ceremonies were held on July 4, 1954, when 64 climbers reached the summit and 40 others par-

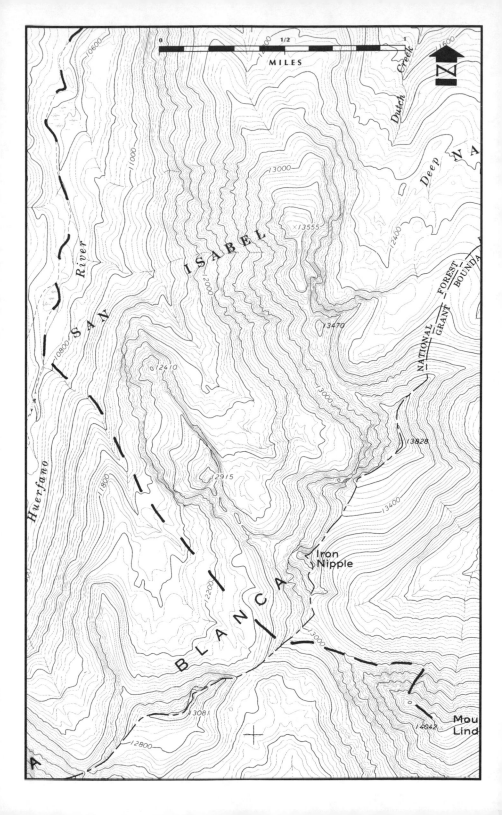

ticipated in the ceremonies at a marker on Highway 160, all in commemoration of a great Fourteener, and more importantly, a great Coloradoan.

THE   ROUTES

Huerfano River
Because private land surrounds most of Mount Lindsey, only one approach is available, unless one possesses the daring to follow the long and difficult Blanca ridge to the peak. From Gardner, drive southwest on Colorado 69 for eight miles to Redwing. Redwing may also be reached from U.S. 160 atop La Veta Pass via the Pass Creek road. When approaching Redwing, take care to continue on the main road southwest and DO NOT turn left and take the fork which leads directly past the Redwing Post Office. Continue beyond Redwing for nine miles to the Singing River Ranch and the end of the road for most passenger cars driven by sane drivers. Pickups and four-wheel drives can continue through four miles of the ranch, taking care to close gates and not to camp on private land, to the National Forest boundary and two miles beyond to the end of the road (10,640 feet). A number of fine campsites dot the valley.

From the trailhead, hike south one mile on the trail to just beyond (less than a quarter of a mile) the unmarked Lily Lake turnoff. Here a cairn-marked trail (hard to find on the valley floor) leaves the main trail and climbs southeast (left) along the southern edge of a prominent talus field. The trail climbs up a narrow valley and emerges onto broad flats at the valley's head. Gain the ridge running northeast from the saddle at the valley's head at any point between the saddle and where Mount Lindsey rises behind the ridge. Lindsey is connected to this ridge by a ridge running northwest-southeast. This northwest ridge of Lindsey offers some tricky rock work, but it avoids the loose rock of the route we have always described. That standard cairned route climbs southeast up a scree couloir before turning south up rock slabs to gain the summit ridge just northwest of the summit.

Trailhead to Summit: 3 miles; 3,400 feet.

The Huerfano River Valley also offers access to Blanca's superb north face and to climbs of Ellingwood Peak, Iron Nipple, and California Peak.   ▲

Culebra Peak

14,047 feet (41st highest)

The southernmost Fourteener in Colorado, Culebra Peak misses by less than ten miles of being the highest peak in New Mexico instead of the forty-first highest in Colorado. Appropriately, Culebra is a peak closely tied with the Spanish heritage of southern Colorado, and while not as heralded as many other Colorado Fourteeners, it retains an individual identity which surpasses many of the state's better known peaks.

Culebra's Spanish ties begin with its name. "Culebra" means "snake" in Spanish, and the name probably originally applied to Culebra Creek, and later to the mountain, for the reptiles are far more plentiful along the lower reaches of streams than on the slopes of Fourteeners. References to the Rio de la Culebra appear as early as 1810, but the stream was probably well known to the Spanish much earlier than that. Culebra as applied to the peak, however, has not been found to be officially documented before 1869.

Due to its geographic location on the Spanish frontier, there is a good possibility that Culebra was first ascended by an adventuresome Spanish explorer, but no records have been found to support such a hypothesis. There is an even strong possibility that Culebra was first climbed in the 1840s, for the peak was very near boundaries of the Sangre de Cristo, Vigil and St. Vrain, and Maxwell grants. Culebra Peak was a prominent landmark for the area, and it would not be too unlikely that a Spanish surveyor climbed it in an attempt to define the nebulous boundaries of one of the three grants. Nonetheless, while Spanish explorers or Spanish land-grant surveyors may well have climbed the peak earlier, the first documented ascents of Culebra were made in 1875 by both the Wheeler and Hayden surveys.

As the years passed, the land surrounding Culebra underwent the typical land grant selling and subdividing. The huge grants were quickly whittled down, but gradually a sizeable chunk surrounding Culebra Peak consolidated into the hands of one man. By buying out all heirs to the land in the vicinity of Culebra

Culebra Peak looking south from the first false summit. *Gary Koontz.*

Peak, Delfino Salazar eventually gained sole ownership of the mountain and a large portion of the surrounding land. As climbs of Culebra became more popular, those who climbed it also usually met Delfino Salazar, who graciously allowed climbers access to Culebra and, as an added bonus, often gave entertaining campfire talks on the history of the area. When Delfino Salazar died on May 11, 1958, it marked the end of an era in Culebra's history. The vast ranch, totaling some 77,000 acres, was bought by Jack Taylor, a North Carolina lumber and land tycoon. Long a working cattle ranch, the Taylor spread is only just beginning to feel the pressures of those who seek to develop its potential as a high-density recreation area. Hopefully, whatever development does take place will be by those cognizant of Culebra's role as one of the last private sanctuaries of wilderness in the state — a role poignantly underscored by a reliable sighting during the fall of 1977 of what could have been a grizzly bear, a species long thought to be extinct in Colorado.

T H E   R O U T E S

Taylor Ranch

Culebra is surrounded entirely by private land, and currently the only approach is via the Taylor Ranch. At present (1988), climbing is permitted only on Sundays in July and throughout the Fourth of July weekend. Reservations are not required, but since policies have been subject to frequent change, climbers are strongly encouraged to contact the ranch manager at 719-672-3580 for the latest information.

From San Luis, drive east on Colorado 152 for about four miles to Chama and then a quarter of a mile beyond to a dirt road leading south (right). Turn south on the dirt road for a quarter-mile until it crosses a creek and comes immediately to a "T" intersection. Take the left-hand (east) fork and drive five miles to the ranch headquarters. All parties must park their vehicles at the ranch headquarters and pay a use fee, which in 1988 was $20 per person. No camping is allowed on the mountain. Camping at the headquarters is doubtful and the ranch manager should be asked the status of that when you call.

From the headquarters at 9,080 feet, hike the steep and straight access road east for three and one-half miles to "Four-way," a junction, and then continue east one more mile to timberline at 11,700 feet, where the road forks south (right) to cross the creek. From this point, a cairn-studded hump rises a half-mile due east. Climb to the saddle immediately south (right) of the prominent cairn and follow the ridge south for one and one-half miles over two large and discouraging false summits to the true summit.

Ranch headquarters to Summit: 6½ miles; 5,000 feet.

▲

A Land of Endless Mountains: The San Juan Range

A land of endless mountains — such has been the impression of many a climber who has stood on a central San Juan summit and marveled at the 360° alpine view. No other range in Colorado, and few others in the nation, can equal the territory the San Juans cover — 10,000 square miles of imposing peaks, high lakes, narrow valleys, abandoned mines, and virgin wilderness. The San Juans stand alone in terms of stirring a unique sentiment in the heart of the seasoned miner, backpacker, or climber who has ventured into them.

One of the range's outstanding features is its over-all altitude — no other range in the contiguous United States contains as much land above 10,000 feet as do the San Juan Mountains. Through the heart of this great mass of mountains winds the Continental Divide, which makes a great bend deep within the range. Therefore, river drainages in the San Juans run toward every point of the compass. The Rio Grande River heads in the San Juans and drains that portion of the range which is east of the Divide, and the Rio de las Animas, Los Pinos, and San Juan rivers flow from the southern peaks of the range. The Lake Fork of the Gunnison and the Uncompahgre are the major rivers to the north, and the Dolores and San Miguel drain to the west.

Passes between drainages in the San Juans are renowned for being high and often inaccessible. Consequently, transportation in the San Juans has been a major problem historically, and today, only Lizard Head, Red Mountain, Spring Creek, and Wolf Creek passes provide year-round paved access across the rugged range. The gold- and silver-hungry miners were a hardy lot, however, and the incredible roads which they built across many other high passes have now made the San Juans a mecca for the hardy (and fearless!) four-wheeler.

Geologically, the San Juan Range is one of the most complex

in the state, but generally, its peaks are of extrusive volcanic rock. Near the beginning of the Laramide Orogeny, a huge body of molten rock pushed toward the surface of the earth in the vicinity of today's San Juans and formed a giant blister in the earth's crust. Later, in the Tertiary period, some of the molten rock forced its way to the surface, and extensive volcanic activity broke out.

Before the final volcano puffed its last, the San Juan Dome was buried by thousands of feet of extrusive volcanic material. However, erosive forces of water (and eventually huge Quaternary glaciers) wasted no time in stripping off large quantities of volcanic material. Sharp peaks and steep valleys were carved out of the once rolling upland, exposing the Precambrian rock of the Needle Mountains and nearby Grenadiers and making them some of the roughest mountains in the state.

Numerous small mining camps sprang up in the San Juans in the 1870s, but five towns became the principal centers of population in the richest parts of the range — Silverton, Ouray, Telluride, Lake City, and Creede. More isolated than most mining camps, these towns developed unusually rip-roaring histories, almost living up to reputations established by modern Western movies.

As population increased, so did transportation needs. It was in the construction and maintenance of the mountain roads that the San Juan settlers faced perhaps their greatest challenge. Nevertheless, men like Otto Mears succeeded in building many impossible roads to impossible places, and despite the threat of the infamous San Juan avalanches, kept communication and supply links between the towns open one way or another year-round.

Determined miners continued battling the topography and the elements in their quest for silver throughout the 1880s, but their battle lost much of its momentum after the 1893 silver crash. Consequently, the early twentieth century saw little economic prosperity for the San Juans. Ranching, sheepherding, and some lumbering aided the economy of the area, but the rugged terrain remained an awesome limiting factor. Mining is still carried out in several parts of the San Juans, mostly for the base metals of lead, copper, and zinc. The San Juans, however, abound with more than modern mining — they still retain the fascinating remains of a mining era which boomed one hundred years ago.

The wildness of parts of the San Juans may be being slowly overcome. Since the opening of the Purgatory and Telluride ski areas, aerial trams with ore buckets now have modern counterparts in comfortable chair lifts, and well-insulated condominiums have replaced the drafty miners' cabins. Even old mining roads, once only negotiated by mule trains or wagons, are now traveled in the comfort of four-wheel-drives with padded seats and even air conditioning. Will the largest range in Colorado, the mighty San Juan, undergo the commercial taming of the Front and Elk ranges? Many an old-timer who knows intimately the toughness of the San Juans would say, "No." Nevertheless, a watchful eye must be kept in order to preserve this still wild and wonderful range.

Uncompahgre Peak
14,309 feet (6th highest)

Wetterhorn Peak
14,015 feet (49th highest)

Rising dramatically in an abrupt north face to stand guard over the drainages of the Cimarron River and Big Blue Creek, Uncompahgre Peak is the highest point in the San Juans and certainly one of its most prominent landmarks. While its broad southwest and southeast slopes afford easy access to the summit, the crumbling 1,000-foot north face gives the mountain a striking profile and poses an impossible climbing obstacle.

A. D. Wilson and Franklin Rhoda of the Hayden Survey made the first recorded ascent of Uncompahgre during the summer of 1874, while they were on an extensive study of the San Juans. They found, however, that they had been preceded on the summit by grizzly bears. Indeed, Uncompahgre seems to have been a favorite grizzly haunt, and both Rhoda and Lt. William Marshall, who climbed the peak for the Wheeler Survey later in the summer, reported encountering the noble beasts during their climbs. Grizzlies and their signs were found on a number of San Juan peaks, and eventually their presence prompted Rhoda to write: "When you feel you are treading a path never before trod by a living being . . . if some such vile, worldly thing as a paper collar or a whiskey bottle does not intrude itself on the sight, some beastly quadruped must. . . ."

Undoubtedly, Wilson and Rhoda were also preceded on Uncompahgre's summit by Indians, most likely Utes, who found its summit an ideal lookout. The word "Uncompahgre" is a Ute word meaning hot (unca) water (pah) spring (gre). The Hayden Survey gave the peak the name from the Uncompahgre River which is fed in part by hot springs near present-day Ouray, a favorite Ute camping ground. The peak was described as "Mount Chauvenet" in an 1873 sighting, after a professor of astronomy

The west side of Uncompahgre Peak. *R. Omar Richardson.*

at Washington University in St. Louis, and was occasionally referred to as "the Leaning Tower" or "Capitol Mountain" by miners in the vicinity.

Marshall's August 29, 1874, climb of Uncompahgre for the Wheeler Survey followed the Hayden men, although Marshall made no reference to their presence, an understandable omission, given the competition between the groups. Marshall observed from the summit: "The Wetterhorn, to the south of west a few miles from Uncompahgre Peak, is a shark's nose in form, and its ascent being unnecessary for topographical purposes, was not attempted. It exceeds 14,000 in altitude and appears inaccessible." The name "Wetterhorn" is one of the few Wheeler Survey names which survived. The name was undoubtedly inspired by the Swiss mountain of the same name, although any resemblance to it takes a vivid imagination. The name "Wetterhorn" prompted the naming of a 13,590-foot peak between Wetterhorn and Uncompahgre, "Matterhorn." A rather undistinguished mass, Matterhorn is nonetheless a fine point from which to photograph Wetterhorn and Uncompahgre.

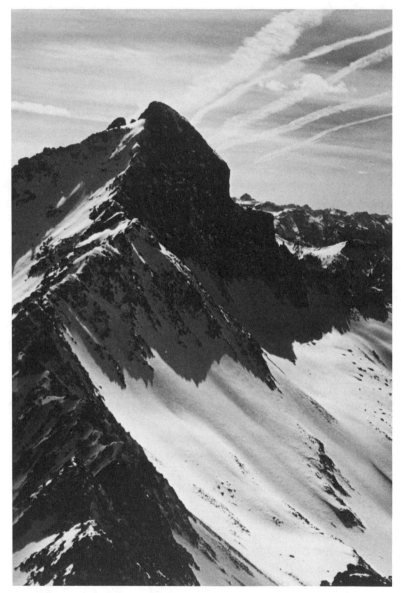

Wetterhorn Peak as seen from Matterhorn Peak. *R. Omar Richardson.*

Although no major mining operations were undertaken on the slopes of the peaks, the valley of Henson Creek to the south was a beehive of mining activity. The chief town of upper Henson Creek was Capitol City, laid out in the mid-1870s. Originally called "Galena City," the name was changed at the urgings of George T. Lee. The Lee Mining and Smelting Company was the nucleus of Capitol City's economy, and Lee took it upon himself, as a leading citizen, to dream of the location replacing Denver as the state capital. Lee went so far as to construct a two-story, brick house with bricks hauled from Pueblo. The house was referred to as "The Governor's Mansion." The Czar, Czarina, Yellow Jacket, Capitol, Sunshine, and Polar Star were just some of the claims near Capitol City. Like George Lee's dreams, the dreams of their owners, too, evaporated with the demonetarization of silver in 1893.

By far the biggest producer of the Henson Creek Valley was the Ute-Ulay mine, located four miles west of Lake City. The mine was originally discovered on August 27, 1871, by Harry Henson, Joel Mullen, Albert Meade, and Charles Godwin, but the miners were forced to wait for the signing of the 1873 Brunot Treaty which opened the area, then part of the Ute reservation, to mining. When this was done in 1874, Henson and his partners returned, and within two years, they had developed so much promise in the claim that the Crooke Brothers Smelter of Lake City bought them out for $125,000. By 1911, the mine had produced more than $10 million in silver and lead. It continues to operate sporadically.

Unlike its neighbor, which attracted outings from Capitol City and Lake City, Wetterhorn remained unclimbed until 1906, when a party of D. Utter, George C. Barnard, C. Smedley, and W. P. Smedley, detoured from a planned ascent of Uncompahgre to climb, in Barnard's words, "a peak that was worthy of our metal (*sic*], both in difficulty and height." The climb was made via the standard south ridge approach. In August of 1920, the competent duo of Albert Ellingwood and Barton Hoag ascended the peak via the east arete. The north face of the Wetterhorn, spectacular from Matterhorn if laced with snow and ice, poses an impossible climbing challenge because of its crumbling volcanic structure.

T H E   R O U T E S

Nellie Creek (Usually Uncompahgre Only)
From the intersection of Second Street and Colorado 149 in Lake City, at the sign indicating "Engineer Pass," drive west up the Henson Creek road for four miles to the Ute-Ulay mine and 1.4 miles farther to the Nellie Creek road, which branches off to the north (right). The road is usually plowed to the Ute-Ulay in winter. The road up Nellie Creek has been improved considerably in recent years and it is now usually passable in four-wheel drive. After the road crosses Nellie Creek and switchbacks up a hill, take the left-hand fork through a fine stand of aspen and spruce. A tall, horn-shaped peak looms ahead and usually brings a chorus of "There's the Wetterhorn!" from beginners, but it's only a 13,158-foot point on Uncompahgre's southeast flank, a fact brought poignantly home a mile or so later when timberline is reached and Uncompahgre's unmistakable bulk looms ahead. The Nellie Creek road becomes a foot trail at about 11,400 feet, four miles from Henson Creek, at the Big Blue Wilderness boundary. From here, a well-travelled trail winds west to the southeast ridge of Uncompahgre and then north to the summit, although some may wish to strike due west and gain the summit plateau just above the obvious south cliffs.

Nellie Creek/Henson Creek junction to Summit: 7 miles; 5,000 feet.

Wilderness boundary to Summit: 3 miles; 2,900 feet.

Matterhorn Creek
From Lake City, drive nine miles west to Capitol City and then northwest for almost two miles up the North Fork of Henson Creek to its confluence with Matterhorn Creek. Most high-clearance vehicles can continue another one-half mile up Matterhorn Creek to a parking area at the wilderness boundary. Hike north up Matterhorn trail, climbing across a broad avalanche run and past the prominent buttress of Wetterhorn's southeast flank. After gaining the pass at the head of the Matterhorn Creek drainage, Uncompahgre beckons to the northeast either by following a trail which loops wildly south, eventually reaching the Nellie Creek route on the southeast or, more sanely, by mounting the summit plateau west of the prominent south cliffs by a combina-

tion of couloir and rock rib. The summit view is spectacular, but have someone hold your feet (make sure your boots are tightly laced!) if you lean too far over the north face to take pictures.

For Wetterhorn singularly or with Uncompahgre, strike out west across the broad basin on Wetterhorn's east side about a half-mile south of Matterhorn and the 12,458-foot pass. Climb into the basin and then southwest, gaining the southeast ridge. The ridge demands the use of hands as it climbs above 13,400 feet. At 13,850 feet, the route passes beneath a prominent shark's tooth point and then directly west through a keyhole of sorts between the main peak and shark's tooth. A series of rock ledges lead the final 150 feet to a small but surprisingly level summit. The ledges are not particularly hard climbing, but a mixture of ice and snow may warrant a rope, as one false step sends one plummeting past the keyhole down the 600-foot southwest face. The view off Wetterhorn's 800-foot north face is equally impressive.

Matterhorn Creek trailhead to Uncompahgre: 4½ miles (via southwest couloir); 3,600 feet, plus 250 feet on return.

Matterhorn Creek trailhead to Wetterhorn: 3½ miles; 3,300 feet.

Matterhorn Creek trailhead, both peaks, roundtrip: 13 miles; 7,450 feet (a very long day).

Beware the drinking water on any summer climb, as the area is usually covered with sheep. This fact, coupled with rather bland and tiresome loose rock, make Wetterhorn and Uncompahgre far more interesting either in spring when snow gives the peaks a more spectacular character or in fall when aspen leaves illuminate the valleys. An interesting summer climb, however, could be made in conjunction with a backpack trip up any of the three forks of the Cimarron River from National Forest access roads leading south from U.S. 50 between Gunnison and Montrose.

▲

Sunshine Peak
14,001 feet (54th highest)

Redcloud Peak
14,034 feet (46th highest)

Topping the collection of rounded summits which separate the Lake Fork of the Gunnison and Henson Creek are Sunshine and Redcloud peaks, connected to each other by a rolling one and one-half mile ridge. Not as ruggedly impressive as many San Juan summits, the two peaks are often lost in a maze of mountains when viewed from a distance, but at closer range, each possesses distinctive physical characteristics which give it more individuality than merely being a Fourteener. Sunshine's summit rises in a unique symmetrical cone which just barely pierces the 14,000-foot level, while Redcloud Peak displays gently rounded upper slopes of a beautiful, dull reddish-orange hue found on no other Colorado Fourteener.

Sunshine and Redcloud are easily ascended and therefore may have been climbed by prospectors in the early 1870s, but the first recorded ascents of both peaks were made by members of the Wheeler and Hayden surveys. In 1874, Chief Topographer A. D. Wilson and Assistant Topographer Franklin Rhoda of the Hayden Survey made the first recorded ascent of Sunshine, which they had designated as simply "Station 12," one of a series of triangulation stations. They rode donkeys to 13,000 feet and then found the climb itself to be of little difficulty, but were confronted with considerable electrical activity once they reached the summit. This storm curtailed their work on Sunshine and also prevented them from continuing north along the ridge to Redcloud. The tickling sensation produced by the electricity in the air and the buzzing of nearby rocks were interesting phenomena indeed, but also warning signals. Wisely, Wilson and Rhoda hightailed down the southeast ridge of Sunshine just as a deadly bolt of

Redcloud Peak (left) and Sunshine (right), from the west atop Handies Peak. *Craig F. Koontz.*

lightning struck the summit where they had been standing only moments before.

Later in 1874, members of the Wheeler Survey also passed through the valleys above Lake San Cristobal and were impressed by the beautiful coloration and form of Redcloud. Realizing that the peak was called "Red Mountain" informally, but had no official name, topographer J. C. Spiller suggested the beautifully descriptive "Red Cloud," one of the few Wheeler names in the Colorado Rockies which has remained. In addition to naming it, Spiller also made the first recorded ascent of Redcloud and established a triangulation station on its summit. Apparently Spiller encountered no electrical storms such as the one experienced on neighboring Sunshine by the Hayden Survey, and had ample time to complete his surveying work on its summit.

In the late 1870s, silver prospectors flooded the valleys of the San Juans, and the upper Lake Fork of the Gunnison was no exception. In 1877, the town of Sherman was laid out at the foot of the cliffs on Sunshine's south slope and a number of mines were located near town. An exception among Colorado mining camps, Sherman never really boomed, and it probably never exceeded 300 in population. The most productive mine in the area was the Black Wonder which operated into the twentieth century, but Sherman itself was abandoned after the silver crash of 1893, and all mining in the area ceased by the 1920s. If one wonders why Sherman never boomed despite its promising mines, a clue may be found in noting the camp's geographical setting. Sherman was located in the flats at the confluence of the Lake Fork and Cottonwood Creek, and nearly every spring, the two streams inundated the town under several feet of runoff water! Undisputedly a victim of very poor land-use planning, Sherman has all but washed away, and only portions of a few cabins remain in defiance of the flood waters.

While Redcloud has been the official name of the peak since Spiller's christening, "Station 12" was informally known as "Mount Sherman" or "Niagara Peak" by miners until the U.S. Geological Survey of 1904-1905 officially designated it as Sunshine Peak without giving any particular reason for the name choice. Sunshine's most recent claim to fame has been its calculation as the lowest Fourteener in Colorado.

On July 19, 1986, Utah climber David Wilson fell several hundred feet to his death on Sunshine's south cliffs. Wilson was climbing alone and had pushed on to Redcloud despite a severe thunderstorm which forced other climbers off the peaks. Returning over Sunshine, he missed the descent route and soon faced rain-slickened rocks and 800-foot cliffs. Wilson was ill-equipped for bad weather, and hypothermia as well as the lack of a map may have clouded his judgment. His body was located two days later, after a massive search. The lessons are obvious.

T H E   R O U T E S

Mill Creek Campground

From Lake City, drive approximately 14 miles past Lake San Cristobal and up the Lake Fork on a good gravel road to the BLM Mill Creek Campground. Park or camp here (9,450 feet), where the summit of Sunshine is hidden by the cliffs to the northwest.

To begin the climb, climb east of the cliffs on Sunshine's south slope by picking your way up the steep talus directly to the north of the campground. Work upslope to the northwest, through the trees and then to timberline (11,800 feet). One-half mile farther northwest, cross the large flat shoulder at 12,500 feet and then climb the rocky east ridge of Sunshine which appears as a false summit directly above the flats, with Sunshine's summit cone prominently behind and to the left. Once on top of the ridge, Sunshine's summit is 400 feet above and a quarter-mile farther west.

For Redcloud, descend Sunshine's north ridge one-half mile to the 13,500-foot saddle and then climb north on the trail which skirts west of Redcloud's southern false summits for another mile to its true summit. Return the same way, but the final summit cone of Sunshine may be eliminated by traversing across its northeast slope at about 13,800 feet. It is important to remember to keep well to the east of Sunshine's southern cliffs, just as on the ascent, or else you may wish you had packed along a hang glider or parachute to complete the final 1,400 feet of the descent!

Mill Creek Campground to Sunshine: 3 miles; 4,500 feet.

Sunshine to Redcloud: 500-foot gain from the saddle; 1½ miles.

Mill Creek Campground to Sunshine and Redcloud: 4½ miles; 5,000 feet (300-foot gain on return if Sunshine is bypassed).

Silver Creek

This has long been the traditional approach to Sunshine and Redcloud, but the trailhead is about six miles farther up the valley from the Mill Creek Campground. It also starts about 1,000 feet higher and therefore is not as accessible a route in the early spring.

From Lake City, drive up the Lake Fork for about 20 miles to where the road crosses Silver Creek, which flows from the northeast. Above Sherman, the road is quite steep and narrow, but it should be passable in cars in good weather. A trail climbs along the left (northwest) side of Silver Creek for about two miles upstream to the junction with its South Fork, about 11,300 feet. From here, two routes are possible to Redcloud. From the stream junction, Redcloud's summit may be gained directly by crossing Silver Creek and proceeding southeast on a steep cairn-marked

trail over tiresome talus up a gulch on Redcloud's northwest slope. A longer, but generally gentler route, which eliminates the endless gravel pile of the gulch, continues east and southeast on the Silver Creek trail to a pass at 13,000 feet. From the pass, Redcloud's summit is three-quarters of a mile and 1,000 vertical feet to the southwest along the ridge. For Sunshine, follow the trail along the ridge south for one and one-half miles, gaining 500 feet above the 13,500-foot connecting saddle. After Sunshine, a short but steep descent may be made into the South Fork from the saddle, but be certain you are north of steep cliffs due north of Sunshine's summit before dropping west from the saddle.

Trailhead to Redcloud (northwest gulch route): 3½ miles; 3,600 feet.

Trailhead to Redcloud (Silver Creek 13,000-foot pass route): 5 miles; 3,600 feet.

Redcloud to Sunshine: 1½ miles; 500-foot gain above saddle.

Descent from saddle via the South Fork to trailhead: 4 miles.

▲

Handies Peak

14,048 feet (40th highest)

Secluded above the extreme upper reaches of the Lake Fork of the Gunnison River lies Handies Peak, noted for its rich mining history and an unparalleled 360° view of the heart of the San Juans.

The exact origin of Handies' name is not known, but by the time the Hayden Survey entered the San Juans in 1874, the name was already in use. George Bancroft has speculated that the peak was named for a San Juan pioneer, but beyond this, no specific details about the man are known. After climbing Sunshine Peak in the summer of 1874, the Hayden party proceeded several miles up the Lake Fork, and Franklin Rhoda and at least one other ascended Handies, with the aid of burros to 13,000 feet. While this was the first recorded ascent of the peak, the men noticed prospect holes as high as 13,500 feet on the peak and undoubtedly correctly surmised that Handies had been scaled by some unknown prospector before them. A short time after this ascent, the Wheeler Survey entered the area, and they too climbed Handies, both teams finding the summit view to be superb for topographic work.

As extensive mining activity was present in the San Juans since the early 1870s, Handies Peak and its environs were well known to prospectors and miners. Formal settlement of the area began in the late 1870s in the valley of the Lake Fork to the northeast of Handies, in the long meadowed area of Burrows Park. By 1880, the small camp of Whitecross had been established at the northern foot of 13,542-foot Whitecross Mountain, so named for the presence of a small white quartz cross high on its side. Whitecross Mountain is located only about one mile northeast of Handies, and most of the mining activity centered toward 12,600-foot Cinnamon Pass and in American Basin, just west of Handies.

Some of the more prominent silver mines which served the town were the Bonhomme, Champion, Cracker Jack, and To-

Handies Peak looking southeast up Grizzly Gulch. *Lyndon J. Lampert.*

basco. The latter operation was on the road to Cinnamon Pass and was so named because it was financed largely by the Tobasco Meat Sauce Company. In fact, Handies Peak was sometimes referred to as "Tobasco," but the spicy name did not last as a permanent title for the peak. Whitecross probably never contained more than 300 people, and crippled by the silver crash of 1893, the area soon lapsed into sporadic production. By the 1920s, production had generally ceased. Today, virtually nothing remains of Whitecross, but in and around American Basin, extensive remains of the once-busy silver operations may still be seen.

T H E   R O U T E S

American Basin, West Slope
From Lake City, drive approximately 23 miles up the Lake Fork. The toughest stretch of this road is the shelf road above Sherman, and while it is steep and narrow in places, it should be passable for most cars. At the upper end of long and narrow Burrows Park, near mile 23, undeveloped campsites begin to

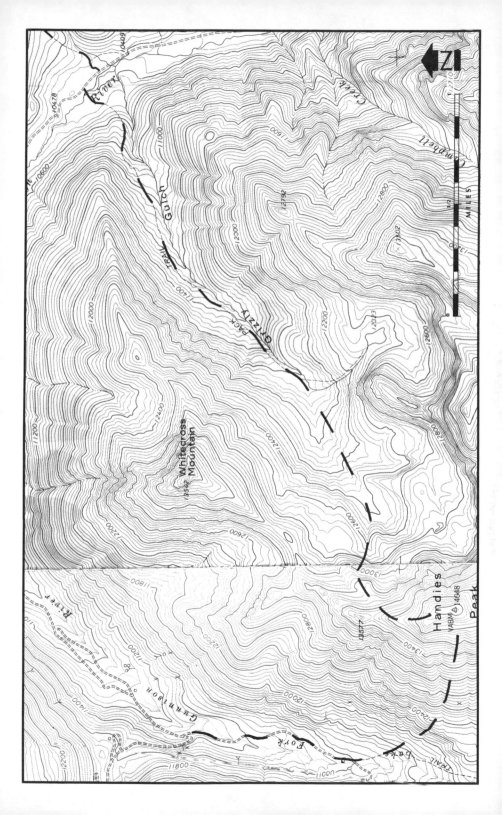

become available in the vicinity of Cleveland Gulch (10,700 feet). The road is adequate for most cars for another mile to the first switchback on the Cinnamon Pass Road, where a side road to American Basin joins. Posted private property restricts camping to either the immediate vicinity of Cleveland Gulch or above timberline in American Basin itself.

For the climb, drive or hike to the turnoff to American Basin at the first switchback (11,300 feet). Directly south at the head of the basin are the imposing American Basin Crags, and bordering the left (east) side of the basin is the west slope of Handies. The summit itself is the highest bump visible on the crest of this slope. Any number of routes are available on Handies from this point. The most direct continues about another mile up the basin to about 12,000 feet and then strikes directly east upslope to the summit, another three-quarters of a mile. A north ridge route may also be had by continuing only about a quarter-mile up the basin and then heading upslope southeast for another mile. The north ridge is a little bumpy but offers no problems for the remaining half-mile south to the summit. Almost any route on the west slope of Handies or a west slope-north ridge combination will work — sight in on the summit and choose your own! Incidentally, if snow conditions are right, the series of slopes and couloirs on the west slope of Handies make for possibly one of the finest glissades in the state.

American Basin turnoff to Handies: 2 miles; 2,700 feet.

Grizzly Gulch

An alternate route up Handies is via Grizzly Gulch, beginning on the opposite side of the valley from the Sunshine-Redcloud Silver Creek Route (for approach, see Sunshine and Redcloud). Grizzly Gulch comes in directly opposite (to the southwest of) the Silver Creek drainage. Follow the trail up Grizzly Gulch along the north side of the gulch for about two miles to timberline, about 12,000 feet. Grizzly Gulch presents a more photogenic side of Handies than American Basin, and there are some fine cliffs seen to the east of the peak. From timberline, cross to the south side of the creek at a large cairn and follow the generally obvious trail west and southwest to a broad bench

leading to the north ridge of Handies.
   Trailhead to Handies: 4 miles; 3,600 feet.

▲

San Luis Peak

14,014 feet (51st highest)

Sometime during the 1600s, Spanish adventurers roamed beyond the mountains north of Santa Fe into a large valley drained by the Rio Grande River and encircled by high peaks. In time, the valley became called "San Luis," after the patron saint, Saint Louis. While it is doubtful that the peak which took its name from the valley felt the tread of Spanish feet, the valley itself became the cradle of a rich Spanish culture in Colorado.

Although San Luis Peak took its name from the Spanish valley below, its early history was more deeply entwined with that of the Utes and Colorado's most infamous winter picnicker. The Ute treaty of 1868 was concluded between the Utes and the United States in response to growing pressure from miners and farmers to wrest more land for development. Specifically, the treaty gave the Utes all of Colorado west of the 107th meridian, just west of Gunnison, or about the western one-third of the present state. The treaty established two agencies on the reservation, one on the White River near present-day Meeker and the other on the Los Pinos River in southern La Plata County.

As the Tabeguache band of Utes advanced toward the Los Pinos site under military escort during the summer of 1868, they halted on a branch of Cochetopa Creek twelve miles northeast of San Luis Peak and refused to go any farther. In an oft-told and hence probably distorted story, the army officer in charge sought to avoid trouble by promptly naming the creek "Los Pinos" and establishing the agency on that site even though it was several miles east of the reservation line and a good 75 miles from the intended location. The Utes and their most-noted spokesman, Ouray, remained at the Los Pinos Agency until 1875, when, as a result of the Brunot Treaty of 1873, they were moved west to the Uncompahgre Valley.

The winter of 1873-1874 was particularly severe, even by bitter Gunnison standards, and it was with surprise that Los Pinos agency officials looked up from their breakfast of April 16, 1874, to see a bedraggled figure stagger into the compound. Immor-

San Luis Peak looking southeast up the drainage of Stewart Creek.
Lyndon J. Lampert.

talized in story, song, and the University of Colorado's student grill, Alferd Packer was fresh from his grisly deed at the foot of Cannibal Plateau. Packer's route from the plateau, just northeast of Lake City, took him across the upper reaches of Cebolla Creek, below the slopes of San Luis, and on to the agency.

Late in the winter of 1873, just prior to the Packer saga's opening act, a Hayden Survey party climbed San Luis' twin to the north, Stewart Peak (13,938 feet). Long thought to be a Fourteener, Stewart Peak was probably named by the Wheeler Survey for Senator William M. Stewart, a prominent figure in Nevada's Comstock operation and a champion of the free coinage of silver. Neither the Hayden nor Wheeler surveys climbed San Luis Peak, although until Mike Foster's thorough research in *Summits to Reach* some thought that Hayden Station 2 of 1874 was San Luis. Station 2 was in fact Peak 13,502, two miles northeast of Baldy Cinco. The first ascent of San Luis was probably by Utes or prospectors.

Activity on the mountain itself has been limited, although

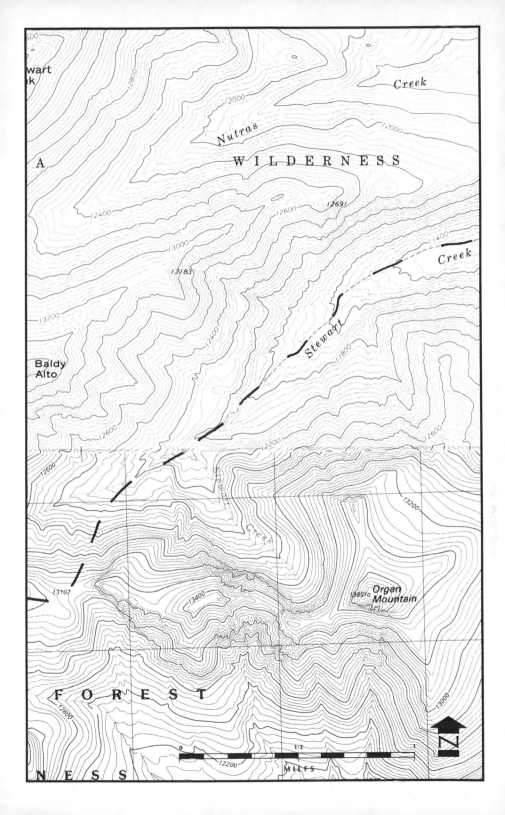

the valleys below have seen their share of ranching and mining. To the north, the Cebolla and Powderhorn valleys offer some of the prettiest and best known ranch land in the state. To the south, men with big dreams once roamed the rip-roaring streets of the mining boom town of Creede, causing poet Cy Warman to utter his famous line, "It's day all day in the day-time, and there is no night in Creede."

THE ROUTES

Spring Creek
Despite quicker, one-day routes, the Spring Creek approach is ideal for a backpacking weekend. From Powderhorn on Colorado 149, north of Lake City, drive south 15 miles to Cathedral and the intersection of the Spring Creek Pass and Slumgullion Pass road. Take the east (left) fork and drive two miles farther to a ranch; obtain permission to park and cross private property to the National Forest boundary. Hike south up Spring Creek six miles to Bondholder Meadows (10,400 feet) and suitable campsites near a prominent tailings dump of a large mine just east of the creek. For the climb, hike south into tall pines for two miles, then east (left) up a narrow but prominent couloir, angling slightly south at its head to the summit. On the descent, take care to return to the same couloir. Temptations to traverse north and descend into an inviting couloir only lead one into a steep, stream-filled canyon. Stewart is a one and one-half mile climb north along a broad ridge.
Trailhead to Summit: 9 miles; 5,000 feet.

Stewart Creek
From eight miles east of Gunnison on U.S. 50, drive south 20.6 miles on Colorado 114 and turn right on County Road NN14, the old Cochetopa Pass road. Three and one-half miles farther, at the Los Pinos Pass road junction, continue straight ahead for another 3.6 miles past the Dome Lakes. At the south end of Dome Lakes, take the Stewart Creek road (County Road 15GG) to the right for about 21 miles to the Stewart Creek trailhead. Keep left at major intersections at miles 8.6 and 16.5 on this road. The Stewart Creek trail climbs from 10,500 feet to timber-

line, four and one-quarter miles to the southwest. Climb to the 13,107-foot saddle on San Luis' northeast flank, and then west and southwest to the summit, another mile distant.

Stewart Creek trailhead to Summit: 6 miles; 3,500 feet.

Backpackers may wish to explore an approach to San Luis via Cochetopa Creek. This trailhead begins at the termination of the above-mentioned Stewart Creek Road, one mile beyond the Stewart Creek crossing. This trail climbs gently for six miles in a remote and scenic valley before mounting a pass on the south ridge of San Luis. It is a fine approach for those who desire something beyond the shortest and quickest way up.

San Luis may also be approached from the Willow Creek drainage north of Creede via San Luis Pass.

▲

Mount Sneffels

14,150 feet (28th highest)

Scattered throughout the Rocky Mountains are certain mountain scenes which unfailingly stir the heart anew regardless of how many times they have been viewed. Among these unforgettable vistas is that of the massive wall of alpine grandeur which is topped by the "Queen of the San Juans," Mount Sneffels. Since Franciscan Fathers Dominguez and Escalante travelled the region in 1776, and undoubtedly even before their time, the Sneffels Range has been one of those places which leads people to pause momentarily solely to absorb the sheer splendor of the Rockies.

Sneffels' first recorded ascent occurred on September 10, 1874, when A. D. Wilson, Franklin Rhoda, Frederic Endlich, and a packer named Ford of the Hayden Survey reached its summit via the south ridge from Blue Lakes Pass. After the rugged task of negotiating the rock pinnacles on the ridge, Rhoda noted with some consternation that they had been preceded to the summit by grizzly bears.

By most credible accounts, foremost of which are John L. J. Hart and William Bueler, the naming of Mount Sneffels stems from the Hayden party's view of Sneffels rising above Blue Lakes Basin. One member of the group compared the great basin to the dramatic hole described in Jules Verne's *Journey to the Center of the Earth*. Dr. Endlich excitedly agreed and exclaimed, "There's Snaefell!" pointing to the peak and referring to the Icelandic mountain near the hole that was described in Verne's book.

At nearly the same time as Wilson and company's ascent of Sneffels, Lt. William Marshall's division of the Wheeler Survey passed through the area and christened the peak, Mount Blaine, after James G. Blaine, Maine congressman, Speaker of the United States House of Representatives, and Presidential aspirant. Wheeler's men seemed to be far more ready to please the men who held the purse strings of the surveys than Hayden's, but again it is the Hayden name which is remembered. (And indeed how fortunate! How terrible it would be if more of our mountains were named for long-forgotten politicians!)

Blue Lakes Pass (left) and Mount Sneffels (right) from upper Yankee Boy Basin. *R. Omar Richardson.*

Close on the heels of the surveys came the first small groups of prospectors who would soon turn the Mount Sneffels region into one of the most heavily mined districts in the San Juans. In doing so, the name "Sneffels" was applied to the entire area west of Ouray, and discoveries were reported as being "on Mount Sneffels" even though they were some miles away.

By far the great mine of the region was and still is the Camp Bird. It grew from several silver claims staked high in Imogene Basin late in the 1870s to a multi-million-dollar asset of mining tycoon Thomas Walsh. Walsh took over the claims in 1895 for $20,000 after hearing whispers of gold. He named the location "Camp Bird" after the friendly gray jay. He soon controlled a consolidated property which included 103 mining claims, co-vered some 900 acres, and became the second richest mine in Colorado. Tom Walsh's success story allowed his daughter, Evelyn Walsh McLean, to wear the fabled Hope Diamond. She recounted his story in *Father Struck it Rich.*

The town of Sneffels was organized farther up Sneffels Creek in 1877, beneath the slopes of Stony Mountain. The leading mine of the upper valley was the Virginius, located by William Freeland in Governor Basin just south of town. Fifteen miners braved the winter of 1877-1878, operating the claim in an area which was one of the most avalanche-prone of any in the state. Originally, the Virginius was a silver mine, but rich gold ore was soon discovered as the shaft was sunk deeper, until it was reported that "gold paid all the expenses of production and treatment, while silver is pure profit." The Virginius found its way into the hands of another San Juan mining tycoon, A. E. Reynolds, who in 1884 financed the famous Revenue Tunnel to the tune of $600,000. The tunnel entered the slopes of Governor Basin 2,900 feet below the Virginius shaft and squarely tapped the mine's main vein, solving not only ventilation problems, but also making access far easier and safer by avoiding high-altitude avalanche danger. Between 1881 and 1919, the Virginius and Revenue Tunnel produced a gross of $27 million. Other famous mines dotting the valley included the Yankee Boy, Ruby Trust, Humboldt, Sweepstakes, and Terrible.

The technical climbing history of Mount Sneffels might well be told in two words — Dwight Lavender. Born in Telluride in 1911, Dwight Lavender, and the San Juan Mountaineers which he was instrumental in forming, were pioneers extraordinaire in climbing and chronicling the San Juans, particularly the San Miguel and Sneffels ranges. From 1929 to 1934, Lavender and principal cohorts Mel Griffiths and Carleton Long made ascents on virtually every major peak in the ranges and chronicled their routes, geology, and history in *The San Juan Mountaineers' Climbing Guide to Southwestern Colorado.*

Culminating those exploits were three ascents of Sneffels' imposing north face which involved some of the most advanced snow and ice climbing done in the state up to that time. The pioneering July 1931 climb involved Lavender, Griffiths, Charles Kane, and Gordon Williams in an attack which climbed the prominent east couloir of the north face to the northeast arete. In August 1933, Lavender, Griffiths, and several others did the north face direct via the central couloir.

Perhaps the most amazing, and at the same time the most tragic note of Lavender's career is that Dwight Lavender accomplished all of this before he died from infantile paralysis at age 24 while studying for his Ph.D. in geology. Most certainly he would have been an asset as highly respected and as competent in the geological profession as his brother, David, became to his. Perhaps the premiere historian of the American West today, David Lavender traveled into the La Platas north of Hesperus Peak in July of 1977 to observe Lavender Peak, named for his brother, truly one of the great mountaineers of his or any day.

T H E   R O U T E S

Yankee Boy Basin

From just south of Ouray where U.S. 550 begins to switchback up Red Mountain Pass, drive west on Colorado 361 five miles to the Camp Bird mine (9,800 feet). The road is plowed this far in winter, and once the ice and snow have melted from a spectacularly narrow ledge, the road is passable for another two miles to the townsite of Sneffels (10,600 feet). Follow a trail along the main drainage northwest around Stony Mountain and into Yankee Boy Basin, which is an unbelievable tapestry of wild flowers in June. When the basin levels near its head, leave the trail just before the final switchbacks up Blue Lakes Pass, and then climb north up a prominent, light-colored couloir to the sharp saddle (13,500 feet) between Mount Sneffels (northwest) and its southeastern 13,694-foot sub-peak. Turn left (northwest) at the saddle and, depending on snow conditions, climb a much smaller couloir or its left-hand (south) rock rib to the summit. Both couloirs should be carefully surveyed for avalanche danger.

Town of Sneffels to Summit: 3½ miles; 3,500 feet.

Don't tell a soul, but Yankee Boy Basin has some of the best powder skiing around. Mel Griffiths and party skied into Yankee Boy one night back in the 1930s and reported on return that "none of us were very polished skiers, but a dub would have looked like a champion on that snow." A February 1973 outing by one of the writers found similar conditions, gliding through knee-deep, talcum-powder snow.

Blue Lakes

A popular backpacking route on Sneffels is from the Blue Lakes National Forest access, five and one-half miles west of Ridgway on Colorado 62. From the Blue Lakes, Sneffels is climbed either via Wilson and Rhoda's pinnacled south ridge approach or by crossing Blue Lakes Pass and joining the Yankee Boy Basin route. The technical north face routes are reached via the Blaine Basin turnoff off the Blue Lakes access road.

While Sneffels is the key attraction of the area, it is only one point of a ten-mile-long range which includes, from west to east, Mears Peak, Dallas Peak, Mount Sneffels, Cirque Mountain, Teakettle Mountain, and Potosi Peak. Gilpin Peak, Mendota Peak, and Imogene Pass, separating the Sneffels Creek drainage from Telluride, also warrant exploration.

▲

Mount Wilson
14,246 feet (16th highest)

Wilson Peak
14,017 feet (48th highest)

El Diente Peak
14,159 feet (24th highest)

It may seem strange that with only fifty-four peaks over 14,000 feet and a wealth of colorful history, two Colorado Fourteeners should bear the name of A. D. Wilson, topographer extraordinaire with the Hayden Survey. To be sure, Wilson carried an impressive list of credentials, which included topographic work with Clarence King's Fortieth Parallel Survey, the second ascent of Mount Rainier within weeks of the first ascent, and later, the principal organization of the Hayden Atlas. It was largely Wilson's skill as a topographer and surveyor that enabled the Hayden Survey to establish its highly credible reputation, particularly in the San Juans. Despite these feats, it seems unclear if even Wilson himself calculated on his name resting on two 14,000-foot summits.

During the summer of 1874, Wilson led his division of the survey through the San Juans in an extensive campaign of climbing high points and mapping terrain. (See individual San Juan chapters.) As the season neared an end, Franklin Rhoda, Wilson's half-brother and highly competent assistant, wrote in the division report that "only one peak of which we had any dread remained yet to be ascended, and that was Mount Wilson." Rhoda's reference suggests that the mountain, a dominant landmark on the western horizon when viewed from the Uncompahgre-Sneffels region, was named for their chief at some time during the summer.

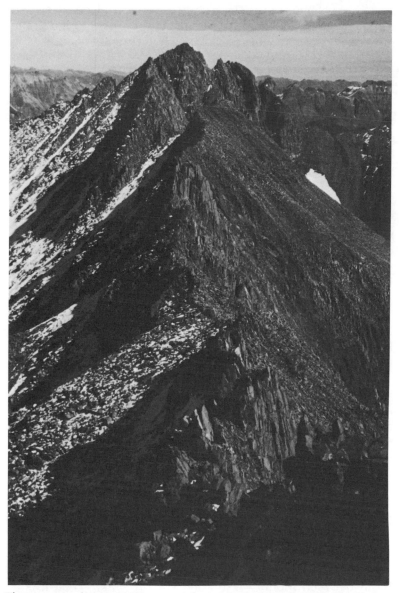

The summit of Mount Wilson and the infamous Mount Wilson-El Diente Ridge, as seen from El Diente Peak looking east.

On September 13, 1874, a party which included Wilson and Rhoda reached the summit of Mount Wilson via its jagged southern ridge. *Roof of the Rockies* recaps Rhoda's report of the ascent, which Rhoda asserted was the most dangerous of the summer. The south ridge of Mount Wilson with a series of sharp needles over 14,000 feet remains a formidable route. The Wilson-Rhoda climb was a first ascent, although J. C. Spiller of the Wheeler Survey tried without success to obtain the summit earlier in the summer. In 1908, William S. Cooper and John Hubbard found a rusty tin can in a particularly difficult spot on the south ridge which bore Spiller's name, presumably left to mark his farthest advance.

As the silver boom of the early 1880s hit the San Juans, Mount Wilson felt the tread of prospectors' feet. Claims were staked all around the mountain, but by far the reigning sovereign of the vicinity was the Silver Pick Mine, located by L. D. Ratliff and others on July 17, 1882, high in what became called Silver Pick Basin. Contrary to its name, the Silver Pick was chiefly a gold mine. Its greatest period of productivity was from 1882 to 1900, although it operated sporadically after the turn of the century, including during the 1930s and from 1959-1961. Production from 1882 to 1961 totaled $682,751 in gold and $124,310 in silver.

The Silver Pick included 13 claims and 8,000 feet of tunnel work on eight levels, all between 12,120 and 13,200 feet. From the mine, a mile-long aerial tram carried ore to a mill located at 11,000 feet. A large stone building which served as living quarters for the miners still stands near the upper tram terminus. Once a haven for climbers, the building suffered the collapse of its roof several years ago.

After the Silver Pick, the mountain's leading mines were the Morning Star, Rock of Ages, and Synopsis. The Morning Star, located in Magpie Gulch at the end of Wilson Peak's east ridge, was a combination lead, gold, and silver producer. While located in 1880, it was most productive just prior to World War I. The Rock of Ages Mine was discovered about 1886 high in Navajo Basin between Mount Wilson and Wilson Peak. While it contained 700 feet of cross-cuts and drifts, its production figures were never anything to write home about. Climbers know the Rock of Ages as the small, adequately ventilated cabin which

Mount Wilson (left) and El Diente Peak (right) with the connecting ridge, looking southwest from the slopes of Wilson Peak. *Gary Koontz.*

Wilson Peak (left) looking east from the saddle above the Silver Pick mine. *Gary Koontz.*

serves as a welcome port in the region's frequent storms. The Synopsis Mine was patented in 1914 at the 12,800-foot level of Wilson Peak and boasted a 300-foot tunnel.

In addition, the Homerhart, Coxey, and Cleveland claims were located in 1905 between 13,000 and 13,500 feet on the north slope of what was then considered Mount Wilson's western sub-peak. Some mining continues in the Mount Wilson area today with the most recent interest centering on copper deposits in Navajo Basin.

With all of the mining activity, miners probably were the first to reach the summit of Wilson Peak. As mentioned, it does not appear that Wilson consciously named two peaks after himself, but rather, that subsequent mapmakers, after Wilson's own 1877 edition of the Hayden Atlas which listed only Mount Wilson, added the name "Wilson Peak." Conspicuously absent from Henry Gannett's Gazetteer, Wilson Peak appears to have been first listed on the 1904 version of the Silverton 15M U.S. Geological Survey quadrangle map.

Despite the high level of mining activity and relative ease of a Wilson Peak ascent, Mount Wilson and its western sub-peak continued to be mountaineers' mountains. In the summer of 1930, after some investigative work by John Hart and others, Dwight Lavender (see Sneffels), Forrest Greenfield, and Chester Price ascended the west ridge of Mount Wilson's western sub-peak. They were confident that the peak's distance from Mount Wilson and the intervening drop warranted its placement on the Fourteener list.

When the party reached the summit, they found no evidence of prior ascent. Lavender duly reported a first ascent and in an admirable show of originality named the peak "El Diente," Spanish for "The Tooth," for its sharp appearance from the Dunton Meadows area. As if to further assert El Diente's qualifications as a separate Fourteener, Lavender wrote in May of 1931, "I actually believe it would be impossible to ascent both Mount Wilson and El Diente between sunrise and sunset even under the most favorable conditions."

A few months later, in an extraordinary case of the keen inspection for which Dwight Lavender was known, he went into painstaking detail to refute his own claim of a first ascent. "Prowling," in his words, through the pages of the Alpine Journal (Vol.

XV, August, 1891) Lavender discovered a Percy Thomas account of a visit to the San Juans entitled, "Mountaineering in Southern Colorado." By comparing the route description to landscape, Lavender concluded that Thomas' description of an ascent of Mount Wilson in August of 1890 with N. G. Douglass was in fact a first ascent of El Diente. Both Lavender's account of his investigations in *Trail and Timberline* (September 1931) and Bueler's subsequent recounting in *Roof of the Rockies* make for interesting reading.

While Mount Massive came under fire from name changers three times, the twin Wilsons were seriously assaulted only once. The 1937 Colorado General Assembly asked the U.S. Board of Geographic Names to change the name of Mount Wilson to Franklin Roosevelt Peak. The Board's response that the name of a living person could not be given postponed the matter until April of 1945, when Governor John C. Vivian sought to cary out the edict. In following Vivian's efforts, *The Denver Post* reported that the General Assembly had selected Mount Wilson to honor F. D. R. because of "its presidential magnificence and because Wilson Peak in San Miguel County already commemorates the name of the 1918 wartime president." Poor A. D. Wilson! With one swoop he was almost conveniently lost to history. The change, however, never occurred.

T H E   R O U T E S

When the campfire's dying embers are stirred and talk invariably turns to a list of Colorado's toughest Fourteenrs, El Diente and Mount Wilson must be placed in anyone's top ten. And too, while far less difficult than its two neighbors, Wilson Peak can be equally unforgiving to the novice who strays off the standard routes.

Silver Pick Basin

From Placerville, at the junction of Colorado 62 and 145, drive southeast for four miles to Sawpit and then two and one-half miles farther to the remnants of Vanadium and a dirt road leading south across the San Miguel River and up Bear Creek. (This junction is six miles west of the Telluride turnoff on Colorado 145.) Drive south across the bridge and at mile 3.3, stay left where an unmarked road turns right; take the middle fork of a three-pronged intersection at mile 4.1; and bear left at mile 6.4 when a road marked "Big Bear Creek" turns right. A total of eight miles, usually passable in sturdy two-wheel drives, brings you to the Silver Pick Mill at 11,000 feet. A number of campsites are available near a series of small lakes southeast of the mill.

For Wilson Peak, hike south about one mile along the trail leading to the 13,000-foot pass separating Silver Pick Basin from Navajo Basin. An increasingly used trail leads from the saddle east and northeast a half-mile to Wilson's summit ridge, staying below and to the south of the southeast ridge. The summit ridge involves some minor hand-over-hand climbing. A descent back into Silver Pick Basin may be made almost directly west from the summit ridge down scree slopes and assorted talus. This descent route may be easier to ascend than the route described if snow-filled couloirs cover the scree.

Silver Pick Mill to Summit: 2 miles; 3,000 feet.

Mount Wilson and El Diente via the connecting ridge is a long day. Begin by crossing the Silver Pick-Navajo pass and contour south past the Rock of Ages Mine at the head of Navajo Basin, under Gladstone Peak's impressive 13,913-foot bulk. Snow conditions may dictate a choice or combination of two couloirs and an intervening rock rib which climbs directly to the summit. Snow exists year-round along the northern face of Wilson and El Diente; ice axes are highly recommended. Indeed, snow conditions are such that Dwight Lavender named the Wilson-El Diente snowfield "Navajo Glacier." A 1975 climbing team reported a bergschrund northeast of El Diente which in spots measured eight feet wide by some twenty feet deep.

Near the top of the rock rib, several hundred feet of extensive bouldering brings one to Mount Wilson's summit and a feeling of awe as he surveys the distance and obstacles to El Diente. The ridge is long and precarious, but of reasonably good rock. Allow at least three hours. Its absolute top affords the best avenue with pinnacle obstacles usually best skirted on the south (left). About two-thirds of the way across, a 30-foot cut is a place where a rope comes in handy for a rappel, but it may be skirted and downclimbed to the south by agile souls. A series of needles, called the Organ Pipes by some, are then skirted to the south before the final summit pull. For the descent, return to a cut just

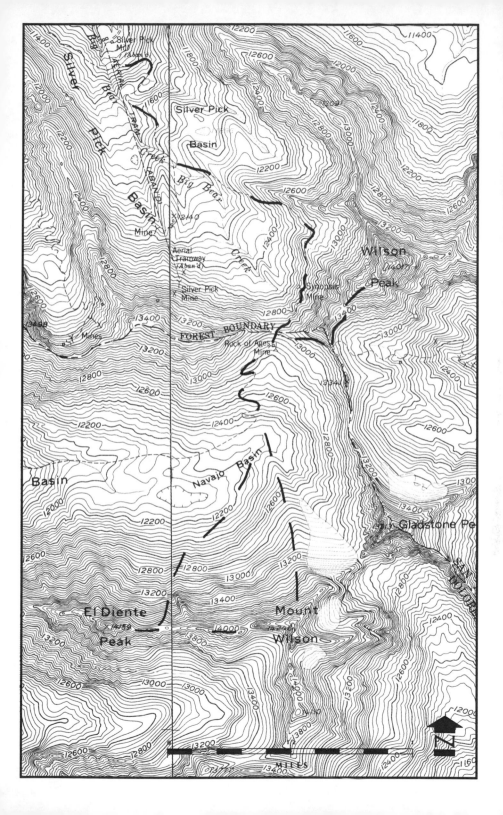

below the Organ Pipes and descend into the couloir running off the northeast face. Then it is a 700-foot climb back to the Rock of Ages saddle. El Diente can be climbed alone from Navajo Basin via the descent route.

Silver Pick Mill-Mount Wilson-El Diente Ridge roundtrip: 6 miles; 4,800 feet.

Jim Gehres recommends this route as an alternative to the long backpack into Navajo Basin from Dunton Meadows. From the Colorado 145 junction four miles west of Telluride, proceed south on Colorado 145 toward Ophir and Lizard Head Pass. Six miles southwest of Lizard Head Pass, turn right (west) on a gravel passenger car road (The Dunton Road) at Coke Oven Creek. Follow the road five and one-half miles to Dunton Meadows. At about 10,100 feet, the road starts to lose elevation and eventually switchbacks down. Take the fairly obscure side road angling to the right and park a very short distance up it where there is a barricade. From here, the trail, at first an abandoned jeep road, heads west for one mile and then turns north for one and one-half miles, gaining very little elevation, and crosses Kilpacker Creek. Roughly two city blocks before crossing Kilpacker Creek, take the obscure path leading to the right up the south bank of Kilpacker Creek. Follow this path until it crosses the creek in less than a mile, and then head up the north bank of the creek across grassy meadows for less than a mile. A fine camping site is located in some pine trees beneath a spectacular waterfall at about 11,000 feet. The upper Kilpacker Creek drainage provides access to the southern routes on El Diente and Mount Wilson.

▲

Windom Peak
14,082 feet (34th highest)

Sunlight Peak
14,059 feet (39th highest)

Mount Eolus
14,083 feet (33rd highest)

Isolated deep in the heart of the San Juans, the Needle Mountains are true to their name, their peaks rising in a spectacular mass of spiny ridges, broken slopes, and craggy summits. The culmination of the Needles are three Fourteeners which cluster around the upper Chicago Basin in majestic ruggedness. Windom, Sunlight, and Eolus are seldom viewed by the casual tourist, and being accessible only by long trails, the peaks remain three of Colorado's vanishing breed of classic wilderness peaks for the mountaineer.

Isolated as they are, the Needle Mountains were long unexplored, and while the Hayden Survey saw them from a distance, their descriptions were shrouded in awe and mystery. On his ascent of Uncompahgre in 1874, Franklin Rhoda received a distant view of the Needles and Grenadiers far to the south and wrote, "in the distance appeared a group of very scraggy mountains, about which the clouds were continuously circling, as if it was their home." Later, from Mount Sneffels, Rhoda again penned, "we have never yet seen the group from any station (and we have viewed it from all sides) without feeling both deep respect and awe for their terrible ruggedness. The fact already stated, that the storm clouds seemed to hover about them before starting their meandering way, only served to add to our other feelings one of uneasiness."

Sunlight Peak (left) and Windom Peak (right) looking east from Mount Eolus across the Twin Lakes Basin. *Lyndon J. Lampert.*

While Rhoda's descriptions may sound as if they came from the pages of *Wuthering Heights,* his awe of the view of the craggy Needles rising behind the precipitous Grenadiers and encircled with threatening clouds is indeed understandable. While neither the Hayden nor Wheeler surveys entered the Needle Range, Rhoda's assessment that the range was a "regular 'manufactory of storms' " gave rise to naming the highest peak in the range "Mount Aeolus," for the Greek god of the winds. Sunlight and Windom, however, were not named until about 1902 when the area was mapped by the U.S. Geological Survey. Sunlight was apparently named for rays of sunlight shimmering through its summit needles. Windom was named for William Windom, U.S. Senator from Minnesota and Secretary of the Treasury during James Garfield's abbreviated administration, in 1881.

Despite Franklin Rhoda's ominous descriptions of the character of the Needles, the area was soon entered by prospectors. In the summer of 1877, Frank Trimble and other prospectors worked

Mount Eolus and North Eolus, from the slopes to the south of Sunlight Peak. The Twin Lakes are in the basin floor. *Lyndon J. Lampert.*

their way to the very headwaters of Needle Creek and into Chicago Basin, where they found promising amounts of silver ore. The following year, the Needle Mountains Mining District was formed, and a number of claims were staked in Chicago Basin, nearly all of them above timberline. In all likelihood, Windom, Sunlight, and Eolus were scaled by miners in the late '70s or early '80s, for despite the rugged appearance of the range as a whole, the three Fourteeners require only moderate bouldering for ascent.

The Needle Mountains Mining District was without question one of the most isolated mining districts in the state until the Denver and Rio Grande came to its aid in 1882 by completing its spectacular line from Durango to Silverton via the Animas River Canyon. At Needleton, the line passed the confluence of Needle Creek and the Animas, only six miles below Chicago Basin. A crude wagon road was soon constructed from Needleton into the basin, and more miners came in. The district never boomed, however, for its ore was not exceptionally rich, and it was still quite isolated, being accessible only in the summer months.

While many claims were staked in Chicago Basin, only a few were actually developed. One of the largest groups of claims was the Mastadon Group which was comprised of claims on the southwest and southeast slopes of Mount Eolus as well as claims about one mile up Needle Creek from Needleton. The Sheridan and Anaconda claims were located on the north side of Chicago Basin and yielded about 12 ounces of silver per ton. In the Twin Lakes Basin, or the Upper Chicago Basin, was the Lake Lode, not exceptionally rich and therefore never tunneled, but nevertheless responsible for the construction of a small cabin near the lakes which still stands in a weatherbeaten condition.

The isolation of the Needle Mountains district doomed it to very little gold and silver production after 1900, and the last gold shipment of any consequence was in 1934. The collapse of silver and gold mining turned the area into the domain of the back-packer and mountaineer rather than the miner, but lately, mineral exploration in the Needles has intensified, now with the aid of noisy helicopters instead of braying burros.

Since the 1920s, the Needles and neighboring Grenadiers have been a favorite haunt of mountaineers, because the area contains some of the most challenging peaks in the state. If any peak in Colorado is yet unclimbed, it could well lie within the wilds of the Grenadiers or Needles. Most new routes have been pioneered on nearby thirteeners, but the three Fourteeners in the range have also seen some new rock routes. The west face of Eolus was first climbed by Joe Merhar, Chris Schoredos, and H. L. and Frank McClintock in 1940. The north face of Sunlight was first conquered in 1934 by William House and Elizabeth Woolsey. Also in 1934, the impressive Needle Ridge, which runs west of Sunlight and dominates the skyline above the Twin Lakes, was first traversed by Robert Ormes and T. M. Griffiths.

While summer climbs of the Needles became increasingly popular throughout the mid-1900s, Sunlight and Windom were not climbed in the winter until 1966. On December 18, 1966, Don Monk, Kermith Ross, and Phil Schmuck began hiking along the narrow-gauge right-of-way from Rockwood, and with the aid of food caches placed in August, reached the cabin at the Twin

Lakes in three days. On December 22, 1966, the trio reached the summit of Windom, and on the following day, they climbed Sunlight. On December 24, they reached the 13,500-foot level on Eolus, but were turned back by threatening weather and a precarious-looking, snow-covered north ridge. Eolus remained unconquered in the winter until January 26, 1971, when Barry Nash, Steve Lewis, Floyd Frank, and Rick Nolting reached the summit via the north ridge and northeast face after snowshoeing in from the Purgatory Ski Area. This ascent made Mount Eolus one of the last of Colorado's Fourteeners to be climbed in the winter, an indication of the rugged isolation of the Needle Mountains.

T H E   R O U T E S

Chicago Basin

"All Ab-o-o-o-ard!" This is how most climbers begin their approach to climb in the Needles or Grenadiers — the Durango to Silverton narrow-gauge train! This is definitely recommended, for being dropped off deep in the Animas River Canyon by an 1880 steam locomotive-drawn train at Needleton is an experience not to be forgotten and it avoids a long, long backpack from trailheads which are reached by roads. The Durango & Silverton Railroad operates from about May 1 through October 30. During the peak summer season, four trains daily run on the line. Because of the numerous schedules, it is very important to make reservations well in advance and then confirm boarding and departure times with the depot in Durango. Policies for backpackers will vary depending on the time of year. The depot is located at 479 Main Avenue and the reservation number is (303) 247-2733. Tickets must be picked up by 6:00 P.M. the evening before the trip. Firearms, pets, and alcoholic beverages are not permitted on the train.

In the summer of 1988, the Durango & Silverton inaugurated a new service for backpackers called the Animas River Railway. A motorized coach with connecting gondola runs from Rockwood, 17 miles north of Durango, to the Elk Park wye with a stop at Needleton and then returns to Rockwood each morning. At this writing, it is unclear how well this service will be received, how its schedules might change, and how it will affect back-packer use of the regular trains. Reservations must be made by calling the Animas River Railway direct at (303) 247-9349.

It is also possible to ride from Silverton south, but these tickets are sold on a space available basis only in Silverton, and backpackers traditionally been assigned to just one southbound train. Times and policies for return trips should be confirmed before departure.

Get off the train at Needleton and cross the suspension bridge east over the Animas River. The Chicago Basin-Columbine Pass trail leads gently south along the Animas for about a mile, and then climbs east and then northeast up Needle Creek to Chicago Basin for a total of six miles and 3,000 vertical feet. Once in Chicago Basin — not a broad basin, but mostly a wide-ning of the stream valley — a key orientation point is at 11,200 feet where the main trail bends south and crosses Needle Creek at the upper end of the basin. There are campsites here and throughout the basin, but expect it to be crowded.

One option is to continue north into the Twin Lakes Basin on a trail which heads north just before the main trail swings south to cross Needle Creek. The 1,300-foot, one-mile climb to the upper basin is tough, particularly after the long hike in, but the beauty of the upper basin and the convenience of the upper campsite might just make it worthwhile.

Another option is to continue across Needle Creek on the main Columbine Pass trail and camp in some trees a short dis-tance beyond the crossing. This puts you in position for the alternative route to Windom, which is described at the end of this chapter. This approach, rather than the one described directly below, makes a logical circle route if all three peaks are to be done in one day.

Windom, West Ridge

From the Twin Lakes (where either you have camped or climbed to from a camp in Chicago Basin), proceed east up the talus slope to the right of the waterfall and into the small basin above the waterfall at 13,000 feet. The relatively rounded summit of Windom appears directly ahead to the east. Keep to the right and gain the 13,400-foot saddle on Windom's west ridge between

it and Peak 18. From the saddle, it is a simple scramble east up the ridge to the summit, a half-mile. While climbing Windom, you may find yourself saying, "Holy smokes! What is that?!" in reference to a high and spectacular spire on the ridge to the north of Windom. Now, don't panic — it's not the summit of Sunlight Peak, but rather the Sunlight Spire, calculated to be 13,995 feet high and first climbed with direct aid in 1961.

Twin Lakes-Windom: 1 mile; 1,600 feet.

Sunlight, South Couloir

From Windom, a prominent reddish couloir is visible which leads to the saddle between Sunlight Peak and the Sunlight Spire. This couloir provides the easiest route on Sunlight. Pick your way down Windom's north face and stay fairly high in the basin, dropping to about 13,600 feet, and then traverse below the cliffs to enter the red couloir. Climb up this couloir to near its top, and then angle left and upward along the south face toward the top of the ridge. Easy bouldering will bring you to within sight of a window on the ridge above. Continue contouring below this window to the left of the ridge and go around the corner of a large outcropping and then climb upward to a keyhole which you climb through and then are within sight of the summit, only a short distance ahead.

Upon closer inspection, it will be found that the summit register is not found on the true summit at all, but several feet below the crest of the huge summit blocks. It is not a difficult friction climb to the true summit, but the exposure on the north side makes gaining the true summit at least a psychological triumph. Standing on the true summit has become traditional, although airy, and believe it or not, on a 1920 CMC outing, Carl Blaurock stood on his head on the summit rock!

While on the summit of Sunlight, you can enjoy the view of Arrow and Vestal peaks in the Grenadiers to the north (13,803 and 13,664 feet, respectively). These peaks are two of the most challenging mountains in Colorado, and as is evident from Sunlight, two of the most spectacular. You may also wish to contemplate whether or not the summit of the Sunlight Spire *really* is 64 feet below you!

The descent from Sunlight can be made via the ascent route

down the red couloir, or by picking your way through the slabs and talus on the south face.

Windom to Sunlight: ¾ mile; 400-foot gain.

Twin Lakes to Windom-Sunlight roundtrip: 2 miles; 2,000 feet.

Eolus, East Basin, Northeast Ridge

From Twin Lakes, contour southwest around the hillside and enter the small, sloping basin to the east of Eolus' summit. Continue west up the grassy basin to the headwall. At this point a large granite slab bowl is seen directly to the right with a narrow ledge traversing across the top of it. Pass this ledge and reach the next one above, much broader, which has a cairn-marked trail and passes below the slab cliffs on Eolus' east face. Follow this route as it angles up to the northeast and come out above a flat area and small lakelet about a quarter-mile to the east. Turn to the west up the slope and scramble up the rocks or up a shallow greenish crack which can easily be negotiated to gain the 13,840-foot saddle between Eolus and North Eolus.

Immediately to the southwest side of the saddle, stroll along the "Sidewalk in the Sky," a solid catwalk two feet wide at its narrowest, and examine the two possible routes ahead to the summit of Eolus. A good bouldering route with some exposure lies almost directly along the top of the northeast ridge to the summit. An easier, but more complicated, route may be negotiated by picking your way up the series of grassy ledges on the east face and will put you within 20 feet of the summit. Dominating the view to the west-northwest are 13,835-foot Turret Peak and 13,972-foot Pigeon Peak; the latter is one of Colorado's most striking Matterhorn-like peaks, as it rises nearly 6,000 feet from the depths of the Animas River Canyon, seen far below to the left of Pigeon. Descend Eolus the same way it was climbed, and you may want to make the easy 200-foot scramble from the northeast saddle a quarter-mile to the summit of North Eolus (14,039 feet), probably not distinct enough to warrant separate status as a Fourteener, but you never know. . . .

Twin Lakes-Eolus: 1 mile; 1,600 feet. With North Eolus, an additional ¼ mile and 200 feet.

From the Twin Lakes campsite, it is not overly difficult to climb all three peaks in one day, provided the weather holds, but such an attempt from Chicago Basin should take into account the added mile and 1,300 feet into the Twin Lakes Basin. From the lower campsite, an alternate route to Windom's west ridge starts toward the Twin Lakes Basin, but cuts off and heads into the basin to the southwest of Windom, cutting to the right of the cliffs of Peak 18. The route then heads north ¼ mile to the 13,400-foot saddle on Windom's west ridge. For Eolus from the lower camp, the basin to the east of the peak may be entered by turning northwest off of the trail to the Twin Lakes at about 12,200 feet, well before the lakes themselves are reached.

Appendix

The 53 or 54 Issue Resolved:
But Still, Just What is a Fourteener?

What is a Fourteener? When we posed this question in the first edition in 1978, the debate of how many *separate* Colorado Fourteeners there were centered around Ellingwood Peak. One-half mile west of Blanca Peak and rising 342 (± 20 feet) above the connecting saddle, Ellingwood was or was not a separate mountain depending on the criteria applied and the authority subscribed. Since then, both the U.S. Geological Survey and the Colorado Mountain Club have included Ellingwood in Fourteener ranks.

Ellingwood's presence in the Fourteener club and the current answer that there are 54 Fourteeners in Colorado to the contrary, there will always be an ongoing debate on what constitutes a *separate* summit. Quantitative standards may be laudable goals, but when one considers that a 300-foot elevation drop standard would demote North Maroon Peak and El Diente Peak from the Fourteener list, the debate becomes emotionally charged.

One of the most recent and thorough discussions of peak criteria is found in Mike Garratt and Bob Martin's *Colorado's High Thirteeners, A Climbing and Hiking Guide*. Garratt and Martin apply a strict 300-foot saddle drop, which has the effect of boosting newly named Challenger Point on Kit Carson Peak into the Fourteener ranks — if one is to believe the accuracy of a survey showing the vertical drop of the saddle to be 301 feet *and* ignore any requirement of horizontal distance. Challenger's .2-mile distance from Kit Carson's main summit and the very name Challenger *Point* should be enough to quell any talk of 55 Fourteeners!

The following list of Colorado Fourteeners includes their most recent elevations from the named U.S.G.S. maps. The maps reproduced in the guide include some older 15 minute quads and are not necessarily these maps. Following the list of Fourteeners is a list of subsidiary points which rise above 14,000 feet. The saddle drops and distances from the main peak are listed and compared with the statistics for some of the peaks already accepted as separate Fourteeners. While perhaps interesting, the numbers themselves should never overshadow the peaks.

Rank	Peak	Elevation in Feet	Elevation in Meters	Quadrangle
1.	Mount Elbert	14,433	(4,399)	Mt. Elbert 7½'
2.	Mount Massive	14,421	(4,395)	Mt. Massive 7½'
3.	Mount Harvard	14,420	(4,395)	Mt. Harvard 7½'
4.	Blanca Peak	14,345	(4,372)	Blanca Pk. 7½'
5.	La Plata Peak	14,336	(4,369)	Mt. Elbert 7½'
6.	Uncompahgre Peak	14,309	(4,361)	Uncompahgre Pk. 7½'
7.	Crestone Peak	14,294	(4,357)	Crestone Pk. 7½'
8.	Mount Lincoln	14,286	(4,354)	Alma 7½'
9.	Grays Peak	14,270	(4,349)	Grays Pk. 7½'
10.	Mount Antero	14,269	(4,349)	Mt. Antero 7½'
11.	Torreys Peak	14,267	(4,348)	Grays Pk. 7½'
12.	Castle Peak	14,265	(4,348)	Hayden Pk. 7½'
13.	Quandary Peak	14,265	(4,348)	Breckenridge 7½'
14.	Mount Evans	14,264	(4,347)	Mt. Evans 7½'
15.	Longs Peak	14,255	(4,345)	Longs Pk. 7½'
16.	Mount Wilson	14,246	(4,342)	Mt. Wilson 7½'
17.	Mount Shavano	14,229	(4,337)	Maysville 7½'
18.	Mount Princeton	14,197	(4,327)	Mt. Antero 7½'
19.	Mount Belford	14,197	(4,327)	Mt. Harvard 7½'
20.	Crestone Needle	14,197	(4,327)	Crestone Pk. 7½'
21.	Mount Yale	14,196	(4,327)	Mt. Yale 7½'
22.	Mount Bross	14,172	(4,319)	Alma 7½'
23.	Kit Carson Peak	14,165	(4,317)	Crestone Pk. 7½'
24.	El Diente Peak	14,159	(4,315)	Dolores Pk. 7½'
25.	Maroon Peak	14,156	(4,315)	Maroon Bells 7½'
26.	Tabeguache Mountain	14,155	(4,314)	St. Elmo 7½'
27.	Mount Oxford	14,153	(4,314)	Mt. Harvard 7½'
28.	Mount Sneffels	14,150	(4,313)	Mt. Sneffels 7½'
29.	Mount Democrat	14,148	(4,312)	Climax 7½'
30.	Capitol Peak	14,130	(4,307)	Capitol Pk. 7½'
31.	Pikes Peak	14,109	(4,300)	Pikes Peak 7½'
32.	Snowmass Mountain	14,092	(4,295)	Snowmass Mtn. 7½'

33.	Mount Eolus	14,083	(4,292)	Columbine Pass 7½'
34.	Windom Peak	14,082	(4,292)	Columbine Pass 7½'
35.	Mount Columbia	14,073	(4,289)	Mt. Harvard 7½'
36.	Missouri Mountain	14,067	(4,287)	Winfield 7½'
37.	Humboldt Peak	14,064	(4,286)	Crestone Pk. 7½'
38.	Mount Bierstadt	14,060	(4,285)	Mt. Evans 7½'
39.	Sunlight Peak	14,059	(4,285)	Storm King Pk. 7½'
40.	Handies Peak	14,048	(4,282)	Handies Pk. 7½'
41.	Culebra Peak	14,047	(4,281)	Culebra Pk. 7½'
42.	Mount Lindsey	14,042	(4,280)	Blanca Pk. 7½'
43.	Ellingwood Peak	14,042	(4,280)	Blanca Pk. 7½'
44.	Little Bear Peak	14,037	(4,278)	Blanca Pk. 7½'
45.	Mount Sherman	14,036	(4,278)	Mt. Sherman 7½'
46.	Redcloud Peak	14,034	(4,277)	Redcloud Pk. 7½'
47.	Pyramid Peak	14,018	(4,272)	Maroon Bells 7½'
48.	Wilson Peak	14,017	(4,272)	Mt. Wilson 7½'
49.	Wetterhorn Peak	14,015	(4,272)	Wetterhorn Peak 7½'
50.	North Maroon Peak	14,014	(4,271)	Maroon Bells 7½'
51.	San Luis Peak	14,014	(4,271)	San Luis Pk. 7½'
52.	Mount of the Holy Cross	14,005	(4,269)	Mt. of the Holy Cross 7½'
53.	Huron Peak	14,003	(4,268)	Winfield 7½'
54.	Sunshine Peak	14,001	(4,267)	Redcloud Pk. 7½'

Subsidiary Peak	Elevation in Feet	Main Peak	Miles Separation	Drop to Saddle From Lower Peak (±20 Feet)
Tabeguache*	14,155	Shavano	.8	435
Little Bear*	14,037	Blanca	1.0	377
Ellingwood*	14,042	Blanca	.5	342
Bross*	14,172	Lincoln	1.1	312
Challenger Point	14,081	Kit Carson	.2	301
North Massive	14,320	Massive	.8	260
El Diente*	14,159	Mount Wilson	.7	259
Conundrum	14,060	Castle	.4	240
South Elbert	14,134	Elbert	1.0	234
North Maroon*	14,014	Maroon	.4	234
South Massive	14,132	Massive	.7	232
North Eolus	14,039	Eolus	.25	179
Cameron	14,238	Lincoln	.5	138

* Considered a separate Fourteener by both the USGS and CMC.

The Climber's Bookshelf

The Colorado mountaineering bible has long been Robert Ormes' celebrated *Guide to the Colorado Mountains*. To be sure, Ormes' book is an essential part of any climbing library, and his name is a word for every climber's vocabulary. As a guide to *all* Colorado mountains, it allows for little detailed description of the Fourteeners, but nevertheless, it is a good reference for those who desire brief route descriptions for all of Colorado's major peaks, 14,000 feet or otherwise.

One of the cornerstones of Fourteener history is John L. Jerome Hart's *Fourteen Thousand Feet*, originally published in 1925. A reprint of the 1931 second edition was published in 1972 by the Colorado Mountain Club. Hart's work is an excellent piece of research, filled with footnotes, and is invaluable as a source for place names and first ascents of Fourteeners.

In response to increased interest in Fourteeners, Perry Eberhart and Philip Schmuck published *The Fourteeners, Colorado's Great Mountains*. It is neither, however, a climbing guide nor a detailed history — the pictures are not captioned, and only the barest minimum of information is provided about some summits.

In 1974, a major contribution was made to Colorado mountaineering literature with the publication of William Bueler's *Roof of the Rockies, A History of Mountaineering in Colorado*. It emphasizes, and rightly so, the development of technical climbing; reference to the Fourteeners is limited to first ascents and descriptions of notable rock climbs such as Longs Peak's Diamond and Crestone Needle's Ellingwood Arete. *Roof of the Rockies* is not a climbing guide, but it is unmatched in providing an excellent overview of the climbing history of the Colorado Rockies.

In 1977, *Denver Post* photographer George Crouter produced *The Majestic Fourteeners — Colorado's Highest*. Like Eberhart and Schmuck's work, Crouter's is a pictorial; yet, unlike *The Fourteeners*, all of Crouter's photographs are in spectacular color and are captioned. The photographs are superb, particularly the aerials, but the value of the text as either a history or climbing guide is slight.

Another photography book, *The Fourteeners: The Fifty-Four Highest Peaks* by Roger Edrinn, was published by Westcliffe Publishers in 1987. Westcliffe will soon publish a book featuring artist Bob Wogrin's paintings of each of the Fourteeners.

Other related books published in recent years include Bob Rosebrough's indepth guide to the San Juans, *The San Juan Mountains: A Climbing and Hiking Guide*, and Mike Garratt and Bob Martin's collaboration in *Colorado's High Thirteeners*, which reminds us that there really are more than just fifty-four peaks in the state!

For those desiring to know more about Colorado's fascinating geology, John and Halka Chronic's *Prairie, Peak and Plateau* provides an excellent layman's introduction. Ghost-town sleuths, of course, cannot go wrong if they refer to the old reliable stand-by of beloved Muriel Sibell Wolle, *Stampede to Timberline*.

While a recounting of the numerous sources used in this book would consume many pages, two invaluable sources for anyone wishing to do further research and the most heavily relied upon sources for the present work are the Colorado Mountain Club's *Trail and Timberline* and the newspaper and clipping files of the Denver Public Library's Western History Department. The many people who contributed their knowledge are gratefully thanked in the acknowledgements.

Index